"Recognizing and using English idioms and phrasal verbs is essential to fluency. My students love learning and using idioms, but we can only cover so many of them in class. This series gives learners a fun, contextual way to access and learn a plethora of idiomatic phrases. I'm so excited to recommend these books to my students!"
~ **Brynna Larsen, English as an Additional Language Teacher, Bonn International School**

"I'm pleased with the user-friendly model employed—a thoughtful, well-designed, and systematic approach to teaching second language learners important features of English, including but not limited to idiom, figures of speech, authentic English expression and collocations. I look forward to introducing this series to my Chinese undergraduates next semester."
~ **Michael D. Brown, Professor, English as a Foreign Language, Nanjing Agricultural University**

"A focus on vocabulary, activation of prior knowledge, and the stimulation of higher order thinking are core principles identified by the Center for Applied Linguistics. The TOP ESL books not only support these research-based practices, they promote strong student-to-text interactions in a fun and creative way."
~ **Areli Schermerhorn, ESL, World Languages, and Bilingual Peer Observer, Syracuse City School District**

"TOP ESL is a great advancement in the education of English language learners. Idioms and colloquial expressions were always the most difficult aspects of language to teach in the ESL classroom. With TOP ESL, students are able to learn the meanings behind common idioms and catchphrases in books with attention-grabbing plot lines. This is the type of resource that would have been greatly valued when I was teaching, and I hope that future ESL students take advantage of what is now at their disposal."
~ **David Whalen, Former ESL instructor and Addictions Counselor, Dave Smith Youth Treatment Centre**

AN ARTFUL HEIST

A Chooseable Path Novel for Learning English Expressions

Jacob Jun

TURN OF PHRASE ESL
Night Owls Press

An Artful Heist - A Chooseable Path Novel for Learning English Expressions (Turn of Phrase ESL)
An Artful Heist Copyright © October 2015 by Ji Soo Jun.
Turn of Phrase ESL Copyright © October 2015 by Night Owls Press.
All rights reserved worldwide.

Turn of Phrase ESL
www.nightowlspress.com/turn-of-phrase-esl/

Published by Night Owls Press LLC, Portland, OR, 97203, U.S.A.
www.nightowlspress.com
Designed and printed in the United States of America.

Editor: J. Adam Collins
Production Editor: Andrew Tang
Cover and interior artwork by Rick Kitagawa and Eve Skylar

Practice good karma. No part of this book may be reproduced, scanned, or distributed in any printed or electronic form without the written permission of the publisher, except by reviewers who may quote brief excerpts in connection with a review. For inquiries and permissions, contact admin@nightowlspress.com.

All characters appearing in this work are fictitious. Any resemblance to real persons, living or dead, is purely coincidental. Any trademarks, service marks, product names, or named features are assumed to be the property of their respective owners. There is no implied endorsement in the use of these terms.

Paperback ISBN-13: 9781937645175
E-book ISBN-13: 9781937645168
Library of Congress Control Number: 2015910703

To Justine. I love you a lot, a lot.

[CONTENTS]

Introduction: i
Chapter One: An Arm and a Leg   1
Chapter Two: Down the Rabbit Hole   55
Chapter Three: Murphy's Law   115
Chapter Four: Down to a Fine Art   155
Glossary   223
Acknowledgments   227

[INTRODUCTION]

WITH MORE THAN a million words, the English language is considered one of the most varied and changeable languages in the world; new words and phrases are always being added. Much of this diversity comes in the form of idiomatic expressions: *Ring a bell. Face the music. All decked out. Bad egg. Down to earth. Train of thought.* You hear these expressions in everyday conversation or read them in books, newspapers, and magazines. Idioms and other forms of expression introduce you to words that have many different meanings and teach natural communication patterns, broadening your understanding and use of English. Learning how to recognize and use these expressions will make you a more confident, fluent English speaker.

Turn of Phrase ESL (TOP ESL) introduces intermediate to advanced level English language learners to idioms, phrasal verbs, and collocations in the form of chooseable path novels. TOP ESL offers you what no other books on the education market can: a rich source of idiomatic expressions; meaningful contexts of those expressions in action; and a gamebook reading format that will have you hooked with cliffhangers and plot twists.

As immersive learning experiences, TOP ESL's gamebooks are effective learning tools. Researchers have long shown that learning a language in meaningful contexts can help students become more fluent and improve retention. The gamebook format provides the contextual literacy that is so important in language education. With their chooseable path structure, the books aren't just an absorbing storytelling experience but are also a fun story*making* one. As you immerse yourself in the stories and lives of the characters in the books, you become fully engaged in your own learning.

How to Read This Book

Gamebooks are fictional narratives told in the second person and interspersed with decision points. Decision points present readers with a choice between several options. How readers choose determines the direction of the story. Following the typical gamebook format, TOP ESL books feature decision points every few pages. Decision points are either 'language-based,' testing your understanding of particular idioms, phrasal verbs, and collocations, or 'situational,' testing your understanding of the narrative context—story logic, character motive or behavior, and themes. With more than sixty decision points in each book, TOP ESL offers many opportunities to master new vocabulary and idiomatic expressions and boost reading comprehension and literary appreciation.

How the story unfolds depends on you.

But be careful. Sometimes the difference between the options you encounter can be subtle, and sometimes there isn't an obvious right or wrong answer. *A stranger uses a particular expression, so how do you respond? You are faced with a dilemma and must decide between two courses of action, so which one do you take?* The option that best fits the context of the story leads to better outcomes. A good decision may present you with an opportunity or a bit of luck; a not-so-good decision may lead you down a dangerous path. Whatever you decide, your fate rests on the choices you make as a reader.

Introduction

To enhance your learning experience, relevant idioms, phrasal verbs, and collocations in the text are bolded for easy identification. "Tested" expressions and phrases that appear in the decision points are defined in the Glossary at the back of the book. As a bonus for teachers and students alike, suggested activities and lessons for the classroom and self-study will be made available at www.nightowlspress.com/learning-guide-turn-of-phrase-esl/.

IN *AN ARTFUL HEIST*, you are backpacking through Europe with your best friend, Eric, and a woman you met along the way, Darla. In your latest jaunt, you are in the French city of Lyon—just in time to attend an art exhibit at a local museum featuring the *Girl with a Pearl Earring*. On opening day, alarms and emergency lights are mysteriously triggered, and in the evacuation you lose track of your friends. Eric goes missing and Darla strangely runs off, convinced that something is awry. Over the next few hours, you find yourself trapped inside the locked down museum, alone—or so you think. You eventually cross paths with a slew of sinister figures: crazy goons and art thieves bent on stealing one of the world's greatest masterpieces. You don't think of yourself as a hero, but you know you need to find your friends and foil the heist if possible—all while avoiding discovery and capture.

As you weave your way through the darkened galleries and corridors, you will be faced with difficult decisions. In one scenario, you will make your way with your friend, Eric; in another, you will team up with Darla and several loyal guards; in a third scenario, you will work alone; and finally, you may even find yourself partnering with one of the art thieves themselves.

And don't worry: If you make a wrong decision, there is usually a way to get back on the best path. Use your English language skills, try your best, and you will save your friends and foil the robbery.

AN ARTFUL HEIST

A Chooseable Path Novel for
Learning English Expressions

[CHAPTER ONE]

~An Arm and a Leg

A FIRE ALARM **snaps you out** of a daydream. You must have **nodded off** for a brief second.

"It's just a false alarm," your tour guide says over the shrill, ringing sound. Worried whispers spread in the group, and the guide quickens her pace, leading your group away toward a corner of the gallery. "Nothing to worry about," she tries to reassure everyone. "Please stay together. We'll **move on** to the next exhibit on our tour."

You rub your temples and eyes and **come back to your senses**. Next to you, your traveling companions, Darla and Eric, look around in a daze. You have come here to the Musée d'Art Classique de Lyon, a small museum in the Rhône-Alpes region of France that houses a variety of sculptures and artwork.

As your guide calms everyone over the sound of the alarms, your **eyes wander** to one particular painting on a wall. In the scene, an angry street vendor sits in an outdoor food market, waving his fist and shouting furiously at a child running away with an **ear of corn**. Off to the side, another child crawls under the vendor's table and reaches for a bag filled with the vendor's coins.

You are **leaning in** for a closer look when someone jostles you from behind, nearly **knocking you over**. You steady yourself and watch the man **melt into the crowd**. "Jerk," you say, **under your breath**. Irritated, you **fight the urge** to go after him and **tell him off**.

Soon, you realize that you have lost your tour group and are now trapped in a thickening crowd of tourists, visitors, and museum guards and attendants. You can't really do much except **put one foot in front of the other** as you try to **catch up** with your group now moving into another exhibit room.

You **make your way** across the room and look at the banner hanging at the entrance.

LE CHEF-D'ŒUVRE DU SIÈCLE D'OR NÉERLANDAISE: *Girl with a Pearl Earring*

Well, finally. What we came here for!

The Masterpiece of the Dutch Golden Age. This is the painting your college art professors compared to the *Mona Lisa*. Painted sometime in the 17th century by the Dutch artist Johannes Vermeer, the *Girl with a Pearl Earring* is noted as one of the most famous paintings in the world. You feel a sense of awe and excitement knowing that you will finally be able to appreciate it in person. You just wish it were **on better terms**. The crowds are starting to **set your teeth on edge**. Every few seconds, someone is stepping on your toes or running into you. It is **taking everything you have** to stay calm and levelheaded.

It was Darla's idea to come to the museum today. "The *Girl with a Pearl Earring* is my favorite!" she exclaimed last night when she saw a news story about the exhibition. "We have to go. It's the **chance of a lifetime!**"

You remember Eric's expression. He looked at you and shrugged. He was forcing a smile, but the exhaustion of his face made it clear that he was **one blink away** from falling asleep **on his feet**. Darla knew she had to convince you.

"Please, Sammy!" she sang, hopping up and down like a child. When she grabbed you, her hands felt warm in the cool evening air.

"Look at Eric," you said. "He's about to fall asleep on the street." Eric teetered on his feet and directly into Darla's arms. "Can't we go the day after tomorrow? We'll be so tired in the morning."

She gave you a playful smile. "Nope. You boys are taking me to the museum tomorrow, or else neither of you will be getting any sleep tonight." Darla grabbed Eric's shoulders and shook him violently. Then she turned to you, her hands outstretched.

"Darla," Eric groaned. "**What's the rush**? How about we **sleep in** and see it the next day? The painting will still be there. No one's going to **run off** with it."

"**We'll sleep when we're dead!**" she declared, jumping on your back. You almost fell over, but you steadied yourself **just in time**. All the while, Darla began singing **at the top of her lungs**.

Where does this girl get her energy? you wondered.

You and Eric met Darla while waiting at the train station in Berlin. The train ride to Paris gave you all time to become fast friends. You learned she was an art student from Brazil who **grew up** with a paintbrush in one hand and a sketchpad in the other. She came to Europe to find inspiration from the classical masters for her next project.

"And how long have you two been friends?" Darla asked you as she drew a picture of you and Eric in one of her sketchbooks.

You told her you were childhood friends who also went to college together. After graduation, Eric convinced you to go to Europe for a backpacking trip—**one last hurrah** before you would both **settle down** and start careers. Eric graduated as a business major with a degree in economics. Like Darla, you were an art major, and you planned on going to graduate school and writing a book about the American modernist art movement.

You and Eric started your European tour in Norway and Sweden and eventually **made your way** to Germany, where the great **beer halls** there helped **take the edge off** of traveling. After **meeting up** with Darla in Berlin, you **headed** to France. The three of you spent a whirlwind weekend in Paris **seeing the sights**—the Eiffel Tower, the Louvre, Notre-Dame Cathedral, the Champs-Élysées—and eating amazing food before **making your way** to Lyon where the **wear and tear** of backpacking finally **caught up** to you.

How you all managed to stay sane this far is a mystery, but your mind is crumbling now. Your friends in the slow-moving line are just a dozen feet ahead of you, and yet they might as well be a million miles away. If only you could be more like Eric and be perfectly comfortable in any situation. You always envied his ability to **make small talk** with strangers. Whether on a train or in a hostel—it didn't matter where—Eric could always **strike up a conversation** without stumbling over his words. You, **on the other hand**, find it hard to breathe whenever a pretty girl asks you for your name.

You feel like screaming now. Here you are, in a small museum in Lyon, trapped between hordes of sweaty bodies—all for one particular painting.

Even Eric, who was far from being a **morning person**, was helpless to resist. In the morning, when Eric **rolled over** in his bed and pulled the covers over himself, Darla promptly grabbed a wastebasket, turned it over, and started banging on it like a drum. "**Rise and shine!**" she yelled, **waking up** your hostel roommates.

Plus, Eric had another reason for **giving in** to Darla's demands. The exhibit opening was an opportunity for him to **get closer** to Darla. Soon after leaving Berlin, he admitted to you that Darla's Brazilian accent **drove him crazy**. Eric constantly flirted with her and asked her to teach him some Portuguese. He would even mispronounce words **on purpose** to get her attention.

An Arm and a Leg

You feel a tap on your shoulder and realize that you have been daydreaming again. An irritated museum attendant stares at you. "Get to the **back of the line!**" he scolds.

Around you, people look at you as if you have **committed a crime**. In your stupor, you have somehow wandered ahead and **cut through** half of the line. "Sorry," you say. You shrug your shoulders apologetically and walk back to the entrance of the room.

Far ahead, you see Eric. He looks extremely tired and bored. You chuckle when Darla shakes him roughly to rouse him, her excitement adding to Eric's annoyed **state**. You raise your arms and wave at them, hoping to **draw their attention**, but they don't see you.

Someone behind you groans. "This is **taking forever**."

You **turn around** and see an incredibly **striking** woman with radiant green eyes and ruby-red lips. Chin-length black hair frames her delicate, pale face. She looks at you over her pointy nose. Suddenly, you realize that you have been staring too long and try to **make small talk**.

What would Eric say?

"You **read my mind**," you blurt out. "Opening days are always the busiest, right?" You laugh nervously at your own voice.

The woman doesn't seem to notice. "True, but I shouldn't complain," she says. She looks around. "The *Girl with a Pearl Earring* is the **big leagues**."

You are thinking about starting a discussion on modern art when she **bites her finger** and stares off into the distance toward the main exhibit. "Collectors would **give an arm and a leg** for that," she says.

If you decide to respond with, "Yes, priceless. It's worth a fortune," go to **page 6**.

If you decide to respond with, "I'd rather keep my limbs, thank you very much," go to **page 10**.

"Yes, priceless," you agree. "It's worth a fortune."

The woman stares at you for a moment, making you feel uncomfortable.

Does she disagree? Did I say something wrong?

The woman **breaks the awkward silence** with a stiff laugh. She nods at you as if she approves of your judgment. "Yes, imagine the things you could buy if you sold it." Her eyes **flash** with a mischievous glint, and you find yourself staring again.

"Actually, I think I'd keep it," you say, blinking fast.

The woman looks at you with astonishment as her hand rests on her chest. "Oh, really?"

"Anyone can buy a mansion, a fast car, and vacations all over the world. But a painting like that is **one of a kind**. How could you sell it?"

Your own boldness surprises you, but you **can't help yourself**. There is something irresistible about the woman's eyes. They **draw you in**, reminding you of dazzling emerald stones—cold and hard but beautiful.

"Where are you from?" the woman asks, **looking you over**. "You're obviously **not from around here**."

"California—a small town in California."

"Oh?" she asks.

The way she asks and looks at you makes you hesitate before answering. You have every urge to impress her. "A town near the ocean," you add. You swallow and realize that your throat is dry. "It's where the novelist John Steinbeck **grew up**. We have some of his original manuscripts and notes in our local museum."

"Steinbeck," she repeats slowly. She looks at her nails. "One of the greatest writers who ever lived. Unfortunately, I'm not into literature." The woman begins to tap her chin. Her interest in you seems to be waning.

"And you?" you **blurt out**. "I can tell you're **not from around here** either," you say.

"What **gave it away**? The accent?" she says, amused. "I'm from—"

Before she can answer, another blast from the fire alarm pierces the air.

"Loud," you yell, covering your ears.

"Yeah, obnoxious, too," she agrees, though she now seems distracted, her attention **focused on** something else. There is a small commotion in the Main Hall as a group of museum attendants and guards quickly jog away.

You **take a moment** to look ahead to the gallery where your friends have finally reached the main exhibit—the famous *Girl with a Pearl Earring* painting. Eric's head, **bobbing to the side**, looks like it is about to **fall off** his shoulders from the lack of sleep. Darla, on the other hand, has her cellphone out and is ready to **take pictures**.

"So, what brings you to France?" the woman asks, her green eyes returning to you.

"I'm with friends traveling through Europe. We just graduated from college."

"Friends?" The woman looks around. "Where are your **partners in crime**? You look like you're alone."

"Yeah, funny story. We got separated. They're **up ahead**."

"Have you been to Italy yet?"

"Uh, no," you tell her, feeling a little embarrassed. "We didn't put it in our itinerary."

"You definitely should visit Italy once in your lifetime," the woman suggests. "I do quite a bit of work in France, but Italy is amazing. Italy is **where it's at**."

"What do you **do for a living**?" you ask her.

"Museums," she says vaguely. "There's so much to see in museums all over Europe. So much to **take in**, as you know. I adore museums. And even with the madness here today, I don't know where else I'd rather be right now."

"I'd rather be in bed," you admit. "I'm **feeling under the weather** after all this endless traveling."

She nods sympathetically. "Traveling can be a tiring affair. But don't worry. You won't be here much longer."

"Oh?" you say. You assume the woman is talking about the line to see the main exhibit, but her words seem ominous. "Yeah, I suppose so. The line is slow, but at least it's moving. We'll get there."

"**Cheer up**. It will be worth it. Did you know that the *Girl with a Pearl Earring* is only here in Lyon a short while?" the woman says. "Quite an extraordinary opportunity. Its permanent home is in the Mauritshuis in the Netherlands, but they have graciously allowed it travel to a few museums around Europe."

"Yeah, it was a coincidence that the exhibit would be here when we arrived."

"Yes, interesting," the woman says excitedly, though her eyes lose their friendliness. "You came all the way to Lyon and found the painting waiting here for you."

"My friends and I saw a story about it last night. It just so happens to be my friend Darla's favorite painting."

"How lucky for her! To discover the city's small museum is hosting her favorite work of art—the **chance of a lifetime**."

"That's what she said. She wouldn't **let up** until we agreed to come and see it. It was like she was **on a mission**," you say.

You notice the woman's eyes widen with interest as you describe Darla's excitement. She also becomes more guarded, folding her arms across her chest.

"Are you a fan, too?" you ask.

"In some ways, yes," she says nonchalantly. "But I'm thinking in terms of the value of the painting. If I were the owner of this art piece, I would look to sell it, given how much it's worth."

"So, you're an art dealer," you say.

Instead of responding, the woman stares at you intently, her eyes like laser beams burning holes right through you. You **break eye contact** and notice the woman's thick black coat covering her petite frame. It looks oddly **out of place**.

"Aren't you a little hot under that?" you ask.

The woman looks down at herself, straightening her coat and doing a quick turn. "No, it's not too comfortable, but it's perfect for hiding a painting," she whispers. She **puts a finger to her lips** and winks.

You laugh, **playing along** with her joke and flirting. "Can I help?"

"Depends. How **much of a cut** do you want?" she inquires slyly.

"I'd do it just to know your name," you say.

"Well, that won't **cost you a thing**. I'm Maddy," she says, **holding out her hand**. "Don't tell anyone, though. **Keep it under wraps**."

You feel like **patting yourself on the back**. Your attempt to get a woman's name has finally worked, and you are starting to relax. Before you can say anything else, you feel a tap on your shoulder. You **turn around** to see the same museum attendant who sent you to the **back of the line** earlier.

"*Monsieur*," the man says. "Please **pick up your feet** and go."

If you think that the museum attendant is asking you to keep moving with the line, go to **page 16**.

If you think that the museum attendant is asking you to leave the line, go to **page 21**.

"I'd rather keep my limbs, thank you very much." You snort dismissively.

She looks at you, confused, though also a little amused. "You know how much this painting is worth, don't you?"

You scratch your head. "It's obviously worth a lot, but I'd rather be able to clap and jump around at the same time, you know?"

You can see that your attempt at humor fails—miserably. The woman **rolls her eyes**. "Not **your cup of tea**, eh?" she says. "Oh, well. These days, it's hard to find people who appreciate good art."

"Actually, my background is in art," you say defensively. "I just don't **see what all the fuss is about**."

"So, the world is wrong to hold this painting in such high regard?" she asks, her green eyes flashing.

You are **caught off guard**, and your **mind goes blank**. You start to ramble, wishing you had time to **come up** with a better answer. "Well, it's uh—it's just a painting of a girl. A simple portrait. A girl with a pearl earring. I—I don't know. I just can't get excited about it."

The woman probably **thinks very little of you** at this point. She pulls back her sleeve and looks down at her watch. "Well, I believe it's **worth an arm and a leg**—and even an eye or two," she tells you.

The line inches forward, and you shuffle along uncomfortably. The conversation has **taken a turn for the worse**, and you feel incredibly awkward now.

*Oh, well. I **gave it a try**.*

You hate awkward silences. Thankfully, the woman's cellphone rings. She digs impatiently through her purse and answers the phone with a gruff voice. "Maddy here," she says, before she lowers her voice into a whisper.

You look far ahead to the front of the line. Eric and Darla are now standing before the *Girl with a Pearl Earring*. Eric looks bored, but Darla eagerly **takes photos** and stares at the painting in rapt awe.

You reach into your messenger bag, **digging around** for a map of the museum. You stare at the map to **plot your getaway**.

*If I leave and go around the main exhibit, I can take another route through the galleries here and **beat the crowds** to get to the other side where Eric and Darla are sure to exit.*

You turn to leave the line. To your surprise, Maddy has disappeared **out of sight**. Feeling relieved not to have to say an awkward goodbye, you **make your way** back around the exhibit entrance. A clear path near the wall leads through a tiny makeshift gift shop with souvenirs and bookstands. The floor begins to slope down as you walk past several smaller galleries with other exhibits. One sign reads:

Sculptures et Bustes Romains

The Roman Sculptures and Busts room looks promising. It is just a **matter of time** before your friends will pass through there. Hopefully, you won't have to wait long. Considering how Eric looked, and as tired as he probably is by now, you know he will want to **cut short** the museum tour after they leave the main exhibit.

As you search for a bench where you can sit and wait, you feel someone grab your arm. You **whip around**, startled.

"Sorry! Didn't mean to **sneak up** on you, Sammy."

"Darla!" you say, seeing your friend. "I was just trying to **figure out** how to reach you guys. The crowds are crazy."

"We were looking for you, too," she says. "I thought you were right behind us, but then we **turned around**, and you were gone. Well, did you get to see it?"

You wave your hand at the crush of people. "Like I said, the crowds are absolutely **nuts**. I **ended up** skipping it."

"What? How could you miss it?" Darla looks offended.

You explain how you got **kicked out of line**.

"Oh, I'm sorry," Darla says sympathetically. "Still, I hope it was worth it to come today."

"Totally not worth it," you joke. "But don't worry."

Darla punches you lightly on the shoulder.

"Where's Eric?" you ask.

"He's probably looking for a place to take a nap."

"There's no way he'll find a place to sleep with all of these people everywhere," you point out.

"Knowing Eric, he'll just **curl up** on the floor. Imagine one of the security guards finding him. He'll have to tell them he was **floored** by the beauty of the *Girl with a Pearl Earring*."

Darla chuckles at her own joke, but you feel too tired to force a smile.

"Come on, it was funny," she says, **elbowing you in the ribs**.

The fire alarms go off again, echoing **up and down** the galleries and **drowning out** your voices. The noise is deafening. Darla tenses and pulls at your arm. You resist at first, but she only pulls harder.

"Hey, don't **freak out**," you tell her over the blaring sirens. You wonder whether she is being playful or really scared. "It's probably just another false alarm. They've been **going on and off** all morning."

Darla covers her ears and nods. Her purse drops to the floor, but she fails to notice it. She scans the sculpture gallery intently, searching for something or someone. You **pick up** her purse and watch the restless crowd with her. Everyone seems mildly annoyed by the alarms, but most people continue **going about their business**, staring and pointing at the statues in the room.

Darla squeezes your arm and pulls you close. "Look, I think you should go find Eric and get out of here."

"What about you? We're not **splitting** without you. We should **stick together**."

She ignores you. "Over there," she says, pointing down the hall. "See the guards? There's a situation in the East Wing."

"Yeah, seems serious," you say. You watch several museum guards come together in a small group and talk intensely into their walkie-talkies. They must be coordinating some kind of evacuation.

To your surprise, Darla says, "I want to go **check it out**."

"You sure?" You start to feel adventurous. "I'll go with you."

Darla shakes her head, annoyed. You wonder why she would rather go alone. She gives you a stern look. "No, Sammy," she says, her voice changing. "I think it's best if you go find Eric."

The alarms continue to **sound off**, and people start to evacuate the room. Darla grabs your shoulder and shakes you. "Seriously, Sammy. Go! I'll meet you and Eric outside the main entrance."

You **cross your arms**. "It took me this long to find you, and now you're **ditching** me? We should find Eric *together* and leave *together*. These alarms mean we should **get going**."

Darla turns to go, but she notices her purse is missing. She **whips around**. You **hold up** the purse for her to see. Her hands reach out to grab it away from you, but you yank it back, wrapping the leather strap tightly around your wrist.

"Give it back," Darla says. Her expression is serious.

"**What's gotten into you**?" you ask. "Let me go with you. That way, we can look for Eric together after we're done doing whatever you want to do."

Darla looks over her shoulder to where the guards have now left the room. When she turns back to you, her eyes go straight to her purse.

"Okay, then," she says. "**Have it your way.**"

> If you think that Darla is letting you decide, and you choose to go back to the museum entrance, go to **page 19**.
>
> If you think that Darla is agreeing to let you come with her to investigate what is happening, go to **page 73**.

"A fire, then?" you say, confused. "You think it's a fire?"

"I don't think so," Darla replies, "but it's something just as serious. I **have a feeling** there's **more to this than meets the eye**."

"You're being a little vague there. Care to explain what you think is happening?"

"The fire alarms. I don't think they're—"

A loud commotion sends people running and pushing into each other. You grab Darla to pull her out of the way as a panicked tourist charges into the crowd. You reach for her hand. She **stays put** as you try to drag her away. Her face is frozen. **You snap your fingers** in front of her eyes, hoping to get her attention. She blinks several times, shakes her head, and takes your hand.

You **lead the way**, crossing a long hallway that soon **fills up** with people hurrying toward the museum entrance. Looking back at Darla, you can tell she seems distracted. Her eyes scan from left to right and back again in search of someone or something.

"I need to go," she says, pulling her arm back. "Please, I really need to go. Don't wait for me, Sammy." Before you can say anything else, Darla **jumps into the crowd** and disappears.

"Darla!" you yell, but she quickly vanishes around a corner, **out of sight**. You try to follow her, but the rush of people engulfs you.

*Why did Darla **take off**?*

Stuck in the crowd, you **give up** thoughts of chasing after her and choose instead to **go with the flow**. You **look around**, hoping to **catch sight of** Eric as people continue to be **rounded up** and pushed toward the museum's main entrance. Instead, you see another familiar face. Far from the crowd, near an empty wall, you see Maddy, the woman you met at the main exhibit.

With great care, Maddy begins to unbutton her large black coat. As she walks toward a service door, four men **trail behind her**. They look like museum guards, but something seems **off** about their uniforms. Two of the men barely fit into their tight shirts and pants, and their jackets all seem rather bulky—similar to Maddy's oversized coat. In contrast, the smallest man looks weak and frail, barely strong enough to protect a child's **piggy bank**. Each man carries a large duffel bag.

As Maddy turns to watch the crowd, one of the guards unlocks the service door with a key and opens it. The group exits in a **single-file** line. Once the last guard leaves, Maddy calmly **puts on** a pair of sunglasses and leaves the building with them.

You **take a moment** to survey your surroundings and try to understand what you just saw. No one else seems to have noticed five people leaving the museum through this exit.

The hallway leading to the museum entrance is now congested with people. The dense traffic jam of sweating bodies and loud mouths is your worst nightmare. It is as if the entire building has begun to **squeeze in** on itself. Your **heart beats fast**, and your head throbs. The collar of your shirt feels tight around your neck. The room is **running out** of air. You need to leave now.

There has to be another way out . . .

You look back to where you last saw Maddy at the service door. You could leave through there and find another way out of the museum.

Go to **page 55**.

The museum attendant is asking you to keep moving with the line. "*Monsieur*, **pick up your feet**," the man repeats. "Or else I will have to ask you to leave."

You realize that you are **holding up** the line. After apologizing to the angry official, you move closer to the person in front of you, **closing a big gap**.

"What's his problem?" Maddy remarks.

"Earlier, I was with my tour group and got a little lost. The same guy started shouting at me." You look back at the attendant, and he gives you a stern look. "Today's probably not the best day to be working here."

"Poor guy," Maddy says. "All these tourists must be **getting on his nerves**."

"But he's treating us like we're...**common criminals**." You wink. "Too bad. If only he knew what you were **up to** with that coat of yours."

Maddy grins, her green eyes flashing. "He could have been a hero if he was as observant as you are," she says. "When I'm done here, someone's **getting fired**."

"By the way, I'm Sammy," you say, finally introducing yourself. You **hold out** your hand nervously. Her touch is delicate and surprisingly cold.

"Um, you can **let go** of my hand now," Maddy says, and you blush as you immediately release your grip. "Cute."

You **turn away** quickly to hide your embarrassment. To your dismay, you notice that the same angry attendant is **running your way** again.

"That is it!" he says, his face **turning red**. "You are **holding up** the line again. I am sorry, but I will have to ask you to step out of the line now."

"But—" you try to argue.

"*Monsieur*, I will not ask again," he interrupts.

You see his hand reach for a walkie-talkie strapped to his belt, and you imagine being escorted out of the museum by a troop of guards. You **hold up** your hands in mock surrender.

"Leave!" the man demands. He points to the gallery's entrance.

Maddy covers her mouth with both hands, her body shaking with laughter. You feel your face flush as you duck under the ropes and start walking toward the entrance of the exhibit with the attendant **in tow**.

"It was **fun while it lasted**!" Maddy shouts in your direction.

Everyone in line watches as you are escorted away. You keep your hands behind your back, making it look like you are a **prisoner of war**. Over your shoulder, you see Maddy laugh at your dramatic protest. She playfully **blows you a kiss**. Your **heart races** and you wish you could run back to her and get her e-mail address or a business card.

The attendant **drops you off** at the gallery's entrance and hurries back to check the line for any other stragglers. You think about sneaking back so you can talk to Maddy, but there is no way you can escape the museum attendant's eagle-sharp eyes. Darla and Eric are probably **headed** toward the next exhibit by now. You decide you will **catch up** with them at the other end. You smile to yourself as you think about Maddy's green eyes.

*Maybe I can **catch up** with Maddy...*

You walk as quickly as you can. "Excuse me," you say repeatedly as you bump into people. You take deep, impatient breaths, letting the air out slowly through the corners of your mouth. You are busy dodging the massive crowd when a burly museum guard walks directly into your path. He collides with you, his face ramming into your chest. The impact **knocks you** to the floor.

"I am very sorry, *monsieur*!" the man says, leaning over and **offering you a hand**. He asks you if you are okay, speaking quickly while he continues to apologize. You immediately notice that his French accent is one of the worst you have ever heard.

"No problem," you mumble.

You bristle as his hands dart all over you, patting you on the back and **dusting off** your jacket. Then, without another word, he **turns around** and disappears into the crowd.

Annoyed as you are, you decide to call your friends and schedule an early exit. You would rather not stay in the museum any longer than you have to—not even for the *Girl with a Pearl Earring*. You check your pockets, looking for your phone, but you **come up empty-handed**.

A visitor who has been observing you remarks, "Wow. You've **been taken for a ride!**"

If you think that the tourist is saying the man who bumped into you stole your wallet and phone, go to **page 24**.

If you think that the tourist is commenting on how you fell hard on the ground when the man ran into you, go to **page 72**.

Darla is letting you decide, and you choose to go back to the museum entrance. "Okay," you say. "The fire alarm isn't **switching off**, so I say we should find Eric and leave. Now."

Darla scowls at you. "My purse, Sammy. I'll meet you *after* I **find out** what's happening."

"You told me I could **have it my way**," you remind her.

"I meant you could go with me. You said that's what you wanted, so I agreed to let you have it your way."

"Well, I **change my mind**," you say, trying not to sound confused. "I really think we should go."

"Fine," Darla says, **giving in**. She sighs. "I'll phone Eric, and we'll **call it day** and get out of here." Darla reaches into her pocket and pulls out her cellphone. She looks confused as she looks at the screen.

"What's wrong?" you ask.

"No service."

The fire alarm stops. A voice announces over the speakers that remaining visitors should begin walking calmly to the main entrance of the museum. Curiously, the voice tells people not to use any of the emergency exits. In the sculpture room, you pull Darla toward a large statue. You stop while you dig through your pockets and look for your phone.

"Do you have service?" Darla asks hurriedly.

"Wait, I can't find my phone," you tell her, now checking your messenger bag.

Suddenly, the museum lights **turn off**. The alarm starts ringing again—this time much louder than before. Museum attendants **turn on** their flashlights, calling on everyone to walk out of the room as calmly as possible. All around you, cellphones **light up**, casting shadows all over the room as people use the bright screens to see in the dark.

Darla squeezes your arm. The look on her face tells you she has **made up her mind** about staying inside the museum. "I think you should go," she says.

"Wait a minute. Are you serious?"

Eventually, a soft hum fills the air. The lights **come back on**, though much dimmer than before. You look at the startled faces around you. A nearby attendant asks that everyone remain focused on leaving the museum safely, but people continue to shout and shove their way forward.

"**Out of the way!**" someone yells behind you. The crowd begins to **fall like dominoes**, and you brace yourself as a person pushes you from behind. Someone steps hard on your foot. Then an elbow grazes your chest, nearly **clipping you** on the chin. Claustrophobia starts to **set in**. Any minute, it seems, the crowd could really panic and get violent. The frightening possibility of a stampede **comes to mind**. You **picture** crushed bodies on the floor. If there is an actual fire, it could be a disaster.

As your **heart races**, you are tempted to heed Darla's advice and just leave without her.

"Things just **got real** here," Darla says, looking around.

If you think that Darla is saying something serious is happening in the museum, and you should be cautious, go to **page 14**.

If you think that Darla is telling you it is time to get serious about exploring the incident in the museum, go to **page 26**.

The museum attendant is asking you to leave the line. When you start to leave, the man gives you a confused look. "Where are you going?" he asks.

"You told me to **pick up** my feet and leave," you answer with an annoyed look.

"I meant for you to move forward in line, but with that **kind of attitude**, you can keep on moving then," he says pointedly.

Maddy covers her mouth and laughs as you shrug and give her an apologetic look. The guard shakes his head at you as you walk back to the entrance. With your pride hurt, you decide to **take a break** from searching for your friends the old-fashioned way. Maybe it is time to use those precious international cellphone minutes to call them.

You reach into your pocket for your phone.

What the . . .

Your pockets are empty. Both your wallet and phone are gone! Your mind starts reeling. The day is just getting worse. You try to think: *Did I lose them somewhere inside the museum? Did I leave them on the bus or at the hostel?*

Your only option is to **head over** to the Guest Services booth and check their **lost and found**.

Out of the **corner of your eye**, you see Darla run past you, **quick as lightning**. You recognize her by her bright red jacket and the black canvas purse she carries on her shoulder. Darla's athletic frame slinks easily through the hordes of tourists. You **spring into action** to **catch up** to her. Weaving and dodging like a cat, Darla **darts** further and further away. All you can see is her ponytail bobbing in the crowd. She finally stops near a group of people blocking her way forward.

"There you are," she says when you **catch up** to her. "I was wondering where you were."

Even though she sounds happy to see you, her eyes **tell a different story**. They look worried as she looks around the room.

"Eric and I started looking for you, but then he decided to wait in one of the galleries in case you walked by."

"I've been looking for you too," you tell her. You explain what happened at the exhibit hall when the guard told you to leave. You also mention that you lost your wallet and phone.

"I'm so sorry," she says, giving you a sympathetic look. "Maybe you left it back at the hostel."

"I hope so."

"I'm sure you'll find it somewhere. Did you have a lot of cash in your wallet?"

"No, which is a good thing, but I'm going to have to cancel all my traveler's checks." You rub your forehead. "I'm so tired and frustrated," you say, groaning. "You **owe me big time** for dragging me out here today."

"I'll **make it up** to you, I promise," Darla says with a weak smile. She lightly punches your shoulder.

The fire alarm **goes off again** and continues for a few seconds, filling the air with ear-piercing honks and squeals. When it finally stops, all of the lights in the museum **go out** for a few seconds, leaving everyone in the dark. A few moments pass before the emergency lights **kick in** and switch on. "Well, that's new," you remark.

The alarms have been **going off** all day, but so far no one has **paid them much mind**. With the emergency lights turning on and the dim lighting casting shadows all over the room, murmurs of worry start to spread through the crowd. Museum officials begin to direct everyone toward the main entrance.

"Oh, perfect," you say, relieved. You can finally leave this place and work on finding your wallet and phone. To your confusion, Darla **hangs back**.

"I can't leave," she tells you. "I have to—"

The alarms begin to **sound off** again and much louder this time.

"I'm staying!" Darla shouts. She backs away from you, but she stops when you grab her arm.

An Arm and a Leg

"Don't you hear the alarms?"

"There's something I have to **check out**," she tells you.

"We can always come back tomorrow," you tell her.

"No. Go find Eric and wait for me at the front entrance," she instructs.

She pats your hand and **gives you a look** that tells you she is being completely serious. You wonder what painting or sculpture is so important that she has to see it now.

People push past the both of you, rushing to leave the room. Darla lets you go, and you shout, "What if I don't find him? It's not like I can call either of you. Maybe I should just go with you."

Darla pauses to think for a moment before she dismisses you. "I **won't be long**. I'll see you soon."

She tries to move away, but there are too many people blocking her. One tourist, not **paying attention** to where he is going, runs right into Darla, causing her to drop her purse. You **pick it up** and call after her as she squeezes her way through.

You can tell that she is **torn** between leaving and coming back. "I need that," she says, pointing at her purse.

"Come and get it," you tell her, hoping she will come back and leave the museum with you. "At least, tell me what you're doing."

"Fine," Darla shouts. "Bring me my purse."

You **catch up** to Darla and **hand it** to her. She stares at you for a second. "Sammy, if you come with me, you'll be **biting off more than you can chew**."

If you think that Darla is planning on finding a place to eat, go to **page 28**.

If you think that Darla is saying things could get more dangerous, go to **page 73**.

The tourist is saying the man who bumped into you stole your wallet and phone. You glare at him as he **laughs at your expense**. Others begin to stop and wonder what is happening.

"That guy just got pickpocketed!" he tells the murmuring crowd. "He's **been taken for a ride!**"

Yeah, and by a museum guard.

You realize that the man with the bad accent must have taken your cell phone and wallet while he was **helping you up** after your tumble. You can't let him **get away** with this. At the very least, you have to **give him a piece of your mind**. You decide to go after him.

The chase leads you deep into the West Wing of the museum and further away from your friends. You jump onto a bench to see over the crowd. You spot the man far ahead, walking swiftly toward a gift shop. You hop off the bench and **head that way**. At an alcove, you climb onto a pedestal to get a better view of the entire floor. In a normal situation, you **would never dream of** using a statue as a **lookout point**, but you are desperate to find the man and retrieve your belongings.

Shuffling movement along the wall attracts your attention. Your pickpocket suspect in sight, you jog over to confront him, but you quickly **stop short**. Several other men move in behind him. Another security guard rushes past you to join the group. The ill-fitting uniform he has on is similar to the one worn by the pickpocket suspect and the others.

Something seems off about these guards. *Where are they all going in such a hurry?*

The group of men stops in front of a service door. You are about to approach them when the lights **go out**. Around you, people gasp in the darkened room. You stand **frozen in place**. The fire alarms **kick in** again. A few seconds later, the lights return.

At the service door, the group of men has vanished. While the alarms continue **sounding off**, you shove your way to the door until you are standing in front of it.

*They can't have **disappeared into thin air**. They must have gone through.*

"You again!" a familiar voice calls out.

The museum attendant from earlier approaches you wearing an irritated expression. Before you can react, he grabs your shoulder, **spinning you around**.

"Where do you think you are going?"

Go to **page 43**.

You grab Darla's hand and drag her to one of the empty galleries. "I'll **follow your lead**," you say.

"Sammy, that's not what I—"

"If things are serious," you interrupt, "and if you're going to explore the museum to find out what's going on, then you have to **take me along**. I'm not **taking no for an answer**."

You watch as the last group of visitors leaves the gallery to join the giant herd of people in the hallway moving toward the museum's main entrance.

"Let's go," you say, waving her on. "When you **have your heart set on something**, I know it's impossible to **talk you out of it**."

"I could say the same thing about you," Darla replies.

Overhead, the museum lights blink on and off a few more times, and then the alarms start up again. After a few seconds, they **cut out**.

"Something big is happening here," Darla murmurs, taking her cellphone from her jacket pocket. "Still no signal. Strange. It was working when we first got here."

"We're surrounded by a lot of walls," you **point out**.

Darla shakes her head. "There's **more to it** than that."

A loud whirring sound comes from one of the entrances. You watch in horror as metal security gates begin to drop, inch-by-inch, **locking down** the various gallery rooms. If you don't leave, you will be trapped inside.

"Looks like we can't stay here," you tell Darla. "Let's **hit the road** and go."

"Wait," Darla says, her eyes darting back and forth. "Actually, we might be safer inside."

"From a fire? Have you **lost your mind**?"

"This isn't a fire," Darla says emphatically. "Trust me."

"What is it then?"

"That's what we need to find out."

Darla looks around coolly. A nagging thought in the **back of your mind** tells you that Darla is **keeping secrets**.

An Arm and a Leg

"What are you not telling me?" you ask. "You're acting strange."

"I just want to know what's happening."

"And you're going to do that in a locked room?"

The gates are halfway down. It is only a **matter of time** before they reach the floor, sealing you and Darla inside the gallery for **who knows how long**.

"You have to trust me," Darla says. "But if you don't want to stay, you're free to go." She swallows hard and straightens her posture as she composes herself. "**Ball's in your court.**"

If you think that Darla is asking you to choose to stay or go based on your own judgment, go to **page 30**.

If you think that Darla is saying you should ignore her request and go with your plan to go to the museum entrance, go to **page 45**.

Darla is planning on finding a place to eat. You look at your watch. It has been hours since you had anything to eat. Sitting down in a quiet café sounds like paradise right about now.

"You're **biting off more than you can chew**," Darla repeats.

"It's okay," you tell her. "I'll **pay you back**."

"Huh? **Pay me back**?"

"Yeah, we're going to get something to eat, right?"

"That's not what I meant," she snaps. "I meant things could get a little dangerous . . . given the circumstances."

"What circumstances? What do you know, Darla?"

Darla grabs at her purse, but you **pull it away** from her, wrapping the strap tightly around your wrist.

"Go find Eric and wait for me," Darla commands. "Purse."

You shake her bag. "I'm not giving this to you until you tell me where you're going."

Darla points at a group of guards sprinting out of the room. "I'm just curious. The alarm has been **going off** all day—and now this."

"We're getting out of here together," you say impatiently.

You move in front of Darla, blocking her path. Darla looks at her purse secured to your arm and **stares you right in the eyes**. Something about her has changed. Gone is the sweet, fun-loving Darla you met on the train; she has been replaced by a harder more intense version.

"You have to trust me," Darla says. "I have a feeling this really isn't about a fire."

"You're acting crazy right now," you tell her. "We should **take this opportunity** to get out of here."

With each **passing moment**, the crowd of visitors becomes more agitated. "Why isn't the line moving?" someone screams. As museum attendants **push their way** to the hallway to help **sort out** the stoppages, Darla grabs your arm and pulls you back. People are more than willing to let you pass as you walk to the opposite end of the hallway.

"Where are we going?"

Darla guides you closer to the entrance of an empty rotunda with a high, domed ceiling. You wish you had the time to appreciate the architectural details, but Darla continues to pull you further into the museum—and away from safety.

At the center of the rotunda, you see a large bronze statue of a man riding on a horse. It sits atop a giant pedestal. A corridor behind the statue leads to the East Wing. Next to the corridor, a set of stairs goes to the second floor and takes visitors to a gallery separated by large glass doors. The sign above the doors reads:

Photographie

The alarms stop abruptly. A museum official starts speaking in French and then in English: "Ladies and gentlemen, we **have a situation** on the second floor of the museum. Please evacuate the premises immediately. We regret to inform you that the museum will be closed until further notice. Follow the attendants to the front entrance of the museum."

"Things are about to **go off the deep end** now," Darla says.

If you think that Darla means the situation in the museum just got more serious, go to **page 26**.

If you think that Darla is telling you that it is time to go deeper into the museum and explore, go to **page 33**.

Darla is asking you to choose to stay or go based on your own judgment. So, you **weigh your options**. Even if Darla is right about the false fire alarm, you can't imagine how staying **locked up behind bars** will keep you safe when you are essentially trapped. And safe from what? Your **gut tells you** to leave the area immediately, but you also want to trust Darla.

"Well? **The ball's in your court**," Darla says.

You regard Darla's eager face and decide to **dig in your heels** and stay. The nearest gate soon reaches the floor, and a magnetic bar at the bottom locks into place with a loud click.

"Well, we're trapped now, **for better or for worse**," you say.

"Do you know where we are?"

You **pull out** a museum map. "Looks like we're here," you say tapping one wing of the museum. "Roman Sculptures and Busts." You look around. "These look like statues and busts, and those paintings in the gallery over there look like Impressionism. There are two other sections that connect to this one. They might still be open if the gates haven't been triggered." You trace a path with your finger. "If these are open, I think we can **make it out** of here."

Darla remains silent. She goes from corner to corner, trying to get her phone to work.

"No signal yet?" you ask.

She ignores you. This is the quietest she has ever been during your travels together, and **you can tell** that something is truly bothering her. But you **see no reason** to keep **bugging** her if she refuses to talk, so you decide to **let sleeping dogs lie**—for now. Meanwhile, the gallery is deathly quiet. All the visitors in the nearby rooms and hallways have been evacuated.

"What time is it?" you ask.

Darla answers quickly. "It's only been about five minutes."

Darla goes back to working on her phone when you hear the sound of footsteps. You run to the closed gate and call out, "Excuse me! We need some help in here!"

The footsteps stop. "Is someone there?" a voice answers.

Darla **snaps to attention** and runs to your side. Before you can call out again, she clamps a hand over your mouth. **Putting a finger to her lips**, she signals for you to be quiet and to follow her away from the gate.

The patter of footsteps moves quickly to your position. A security guard appears and shines his flashlight through the bars of the gate and into your eyes.

"*Qui est là?*" he asks.

"What? I can't see. Can you put down your light—"

Darla **cuts you off**. "*Touristes,*" she answers.

"*Pourquoi êtes-vous toujours dans le musée?*" the guard asks.

Weird, you think. *Darla never mentioned she knew French.*

"*Nous sommes restés coincés,*" Darla responds to the guard. "*Pouvez-vous nous libérer?*"

The guard's hand reaches to the side of his belt where his nightstick is located. "*Y at-il d'autres?*" the guard asks, looking cautious.

"*Non! Nous avons été séparés de notre groupe,*" Darla responds.

She glances over at you as the guard takes his walkie-talkie and speaks into it. In seconds, gears whir to life, and the gate begins to **lift up** off the floor.

"What's **going on**?" you ask, but no one answers you. "Darla? Tell me what's happening."

Out of the shadows, several other guards appear. Two of them move to Darla's side, **taking hold** of her.

"Hey!" she cries.

Before Darla can say anything else, one of the guards puts his hand over her mouth. She tries to **fight them off**.

"Let go of her!" you demand.

The guard holding Darla forcefully whisks her **out of sight**. The remaining guard asks you a question in French, but you don't know how to respond. "English, please."

Another guard approaches the gate. "Hey there," he says. "We'll get you out of here **in a jiffy**." He speaks perfect English. The accent, though, is Australian.

"Where are you taking my friend? And what's with the rough treatment?"

The English-speaking guard ignores you and nods his head at his associates. You are quickly surrounded. One of the guards slaps the fat end of his nightstick to his palm.

You nod warily and decide to cooperate.

Go to **page 64**.

Darla believes something other than a fire is happening, and she wants to explore the museum and go deeper into its galleries to **find out**. Fair enough. But you also know that Darla is hiding something because she keeps **dodging your questions**.

"You're sure it's not a fire?" you ask again.

"**Call it a hunch**," she says. "I'd **bet my life on it**."

She sounds completely confident. Before you can say anything else, she points down the hall and gestures for you to **keep quiet**. Darla tiptoes over to a stone pedestal. "Listen," she whispers.

Judging from the sound of the footsteps, two people are walking slowly toward the rotunda. Darla presses her back to the statue pedestal. Beams of light from their flashlights dance around the statue, but you stay **out of sight**.

"What a beautiful museum," a voice says.

Darla grabs you and **pulls you to safety** on the other side of the pedestal—and **just in time**. Two pairs of legs walk right past you and toward the stairs leading to the second floor.

Peeking from the side of the statue's pedestal, you see a security guard walking to the photography exhibit and shining his flashlight through the glass doors at the entrance to the gallery. The other guard mumbles something in French. Together, they pull the doors open and walk through.

The rotunda becomes totally silent again. "Come on," Darla says. "We're going to the East Wing."

You try to object, but she has already started sprinting down the hallway. The gallery space she finds is longer and filled with stone busts arranged in rows. You feel a **chill moving down your spine** as you walk through the room. In the dim light, the carved heads glare at you ominously.

At the far end, you see lights bouncing in the dark toward you. More guards are escorting stragglers to the main entrance. Darla signals for you to **take cover**. You **dive** under a low table near a set of stands. The group marches silently in a straight line through the middle of the long room and leaves **without incident**. You and Darla have **slipped under their radar**.

"Psst!" Darla whispers at you. "Are you okay?"

Surprised, you jolt upright, bumping your head under the table. "I have a bad feeling about this," you admit, rubbing your head. You **peer out**, looking back at the rotunda. The group has disappeared around the statues. "I think we're **in the clear**."

"Then, we keep going," Darla says. "We **find out** what's happening, and then we try the emergency exits until one opens. Get your map out."

Darla squeezes in next to you under the table. With your finger, you circle the area on the map you and Darla are currently in. "This is Roman Sculptures and Busts. If we go here, it's more paintings. Over on this side, it's Tapestries."

"What's at the end of the East Wing?" Darla asks.

"The last room looks like a jewelry exhibit. There are some bathrooms there and a set of stairs to the next floor."

"That's where we'll go. If we don't see anything **by that point**, we'll leave through any exit we can find." She pauses, **taking one look at you**, and tries to keep from grinning.

"What?"

"Nothing. You just look so scared," she says, covering her mouth.

"Well, it isn't every day I go sneaking through a museum, **looking for trouble**," you tell her.

Darla puts her hand softly on your cheek. "Aww," she says. "You're having fun, though, right?"

You shrug. The day started out like a chore, but the past few minutes have **rushed by in a blur**. Besides, you have always wondered what it would be like to have an entire museum all to yourself.

"Everything seems so calm all of a sudden," you observe.

"I knew it wasn't a fire." Darla winks and waves at you to follow.

With its empty galleries, the museum seems somber. Floating heads in portraits stare at you in the low light.

Finally, you reach the far end of the East Wing.

Bijoux et Arts Décoratifs

With its glass cases filled with silver, gold, and sparkling gems, the Jewelry and Decorative Arts gallery feels like an oasis in a desert. The red warning lights give the rare stones a pink glow.

"Last room," you say. "Let's **test the doors** and find an exit."

"**Not so fast**," Darla says. "I think I want to check upstairs."

She disappears up the **flight of stairs** before you can convince her otherwise. In the dark, seconds seem to **crawl by**. A sudden gasp from the second floor **makes you jump**. You grab the railing and run up the stairs. Before you reach the top, you find yourself facing two guards carrying pistols.

"I'm looking for my friend," you say, staring at their guns.

"Here, Sammy," Darla says, joining you. She looks terrified.

"All museum visitors are now being evacuated," the smaller guard says as he holsters his pistol. "You shouldn't be here."

"We, were just looking for an emergency exit to leave."

They both shake their heads. "Tourists," the larger guard mutters. "Getting rid of them is like **herding cats**."

"Your English is really good," Darla remarks. "I bet you're **not from around here**."

The big guard looks disdainfully at Darla and grunts. "Both of you are coming with us." He waves his pistol. "Do as I say and don't **go off the rails**."

> If you think that the guard is asking you to put your hand on the staircase rail, go to **page 36**.

> If you think that the guard is asking you to obey their orders without question, go to **page 50**.

You put your hand on the staircase rail and stay still.

"Move!" the larger guard says, raising the gun in his hand and pointing it at you. "Don't you understand what I just said?"

When you don't move, the guard brings the pistol butt crashing down on your shoulder, sending a jolt of pain down your arm and back. Darla screams and launches herself at the guard next to her, hitting him in the nose with the palm of her hand. When his hand goes to his face, Darla reaches for his gun.

The big guard swivels and **turns his attention** to Darla, but you rush him, trying to block his way. The smaller guard grunts as Darla kicks his shin and slams the pistol into his head. He falls over. Darla puts an arm around his neck and uses him as a shield. With careful aim, she points the gun at his head.

"Stop right there, or I'll shoot him," she warns his larger partner.

The big guard holsters his pistol and laughs, raising his arms in surrender. "Very impressive," he says mockingly.

"Do it," the guard in Darla's chokehold sputters. "Pull the trigger."

The larger guard pushes you aside and walks calmly toward Darla. She points the gun at his feet and pulls the trigger. You brace for the sound of gunfire, but only a soft, empty click fills the air. The two men laugh.

As Darla stares helplessly at the gun, the smaller guard elbows her in the stomach and pulls her leg **out from under her**. She crashes onto the steps and goes limp. Before you can react, something slams into the back of your head and sends you to the floor. Everything **goes black**.

When you open your eyes, you find yourself lying facedown. You lift your head only to watch as the big guard **picks Darla up** and throws her over his shoulder.

"I'm going up to the roof, Willie," the big guard says before leaving the stairs. "**Deal with him.**"

The guard named Willie notices you have **woken up**. He kicks you in the ribs. Your body jerks in pain while the room **spins**.

"Get up!" he taunts, pressing down on your back with his foot. You can hear him laugh.

When you don't respond, Willie flicks his foot and rolls you onto your back. The ceiling swirls. You feel like **throwing up**. As you groan in pain, Willie grabs you by the hair and **pulls you up** until you are standing. He laughs as your knees shake, almost **giving out**.

"I'm going to have some fun with you," he sneers.

"Willie," you say weakly.

"Don't say my name!" he yells.

He holsters his pistol and begins to **roll up** his sleeves. His arms are thin and tattooed. In the cold light, his gaunt and unshaven face looks sunken, like a dirty skull.

"I'm going to **stick you**," he says, poking you in the face with his nightstick.

You try to resist, and Willie swings at you, hitting you in the shins. You scream in pain and **fall down**. Willie laughs as he picks you up again. You flinch, ready to receive another blow. But this time, he tells you to run.

"I'll give you a thirty-second **head start**," he whispers.

You **break away** and hobble down a corridor that leads to more exhibit rooms. You look over your shoulder. In the dark, you see very little. Banners and signs tell you what to expect up ahead, and you stumble into a room, hoping for **cover**.

"Go, little piggy!" Willie howls. "I'm gonna have me some fun!"

Up ahead, a room gets your attention.

Outils Médiévales et Armory

The security gate to the Medieval Tools and Armory gallery has stopped midway, leaving an inviting gap. You slide through the opening to go inside. Behind you, Willie is nowhere to be seen.

"**Time's up!**" he cackles in the dark.

The gallery you entered has glass cases filled with coins, stones, and tools, along with larger exhibits of weapons and shields. Pushing against one of the displays with all your might, you make it crash to floor, spraying glass and shelving everywhere. Willie will now know where you are. You grab a heavy goblet from the broken display and wait.

When Willie reaches the room, you launch the metal cup. It hits him **square in the face** just as he **ducks under** the security gate. He **looks up** and roars in anger, his nose bleeding. He stumbles back into the corridor but quickly recovers and scrambles through the gap in the gate.

You are ready for him. You grab a round wooden shield and swing it at his chest just as he **gets to his feet**. Your aim **hits its mark**, and Willie lands on his back.

"Are you kidding me?" he shouts, seemingly amazed.

While he kicks and screams on the floor in frustration, you slip out of the room to find another gallery.

In the **pitch black** dark, you feel your way around until you reach a wall. You drop to your knees and put your back against the wall, covering yourself with the shield. It doesn't take long for Willie to **catch up** with you. He **turns on** his flashlight. The beam darts back and forth as he navigates the room and searches for you in the dark. You wait patiently, watching him creep around. You **hold your breath** and wonder what to do. In the low light, you see a water bottle left on the floor. You snatch it and toss it behind Willie. The flashlight spins toward it, and you **seize the opportunity**. The **element of surprise** is yours, and you charge at Willie from behind with the shield.

At the last minute, he sees you. His nightstick **swings around**, aiming for your head. Instead, it **connects with** the shield and bounces out of his hand.

Over and over again, you charge at him, bashing him in the chest with the shield repeatedly. Willie screams in fury as he tries to resist, but the surprise and force of your attack sends him stumbling out of the room.

You **scoop up** the nightstick from the floor and run to the downed goon. You stand over him, threatening to hit him at any **sign of trouble**. Willie spits at the ground in defiance but **holds up** his hands in surrender.

"Give me everything you got," you tell him.

He gives you his pistol, and you put it into your belt. "You won't be threatening anyone else with this anymore."

"Oh, **count on it**," he says, squinting at you. A trickle of blood **runs down** his face. "The only person I'm **coming for** from now on is you."

An electronic buzz and beep comes from Willie's pocket, and you order him to **hand you** the walkie-talkie.

"**Take off** your belt too," you add. He doesn't move, so you prod him with the nightstick. Reluctantly, Willie unbuckles the canvas belt and slides it out of his pant loops. "Wrap the belt around your left wrist," you order. He obeys. "Now, lie **face down** and put your arms behind your back."

He grunts as you place the shield on his shoulders and **pin him down**, pushing his face into the floor with your weight. Taking the other end of the belt, you wrap it around his other wrist and tie his hands together. Once he is secured, you **stand up** to inspect your work.

"This won't **hold me** for long," Willie says. "And when I find you, I'm going to rip you in half."

You **take off** one of Willie's shoes and **pull off** a sock. "**Put a sock in it**," you say, **balling up** the fabric and shoving it in his mouth with satisfaction.

You **head back** to the medieval gallery and return with a helmet that you put over his head. "Perfect."

Then, taking his legs, you pull him to a darkened corner of the room. For **extra measure**, you remove a large wall tapestry and **roll**

him up like a burrito. He can barely move now. You hope this will **hold him**.

You return to the main corridor, your adrenaline still **pumping in your veins**. The psychotic guard is **out of the way**, but you still have to find Darla and **deal with** the other guard.

You see a gift shop nearby. It seems like the perfect place to rest and regroup. You decide to secure your surroundings first. You unscrew a light bulb from a desk lamp and wrap it in a museum sweatshirt. After crushing it under your heel, you scatter the broken shards on the floor outside the shop's entrance. Any intruders approaching the area will **give away** their position.

You grit your teeth as you lower yourself on the seat behind the counter. You are badly bruised and **beaten up**, but at least you are alive. Things could be worse—a lot worse. You try to **wrap your head around** what you just witnessed and experienced.

Why would the guards carry fake pistols and attack visitors? What is going on?

Inspecting a map of the museum, you try to **get your bearings** and think about how to find Darla. You jump when the walkie-talkie in your pocket beeps. You **take it out** quickly, your fingers fumbling around the device to **turn down** the volume. Before you can silence the walkie-talkie, you hear a familiar male voice. It is the Australian.

"The main floor is clear," the man reports. "No sign of any museum visitors except the ones we're holding onto."

"And the storeroom?" another male voice asks.

"Clear."

"East Wing?"

"East Wing is . . . a little complicated."

"Complicated how?" a female voice asks.

"Willie and I ran into some tourists, except one of them didn't seem like a tourist. She had **moves on her**. Trained. Almost **took us out**."

"Trained for what?"

"Um, kind of like she was trained to stop armed robbers, if you

catch my drift. Willie **took the other one out**, and I'm going to **spend some time** with this one to get a few answers."

"Get what you need and grab Willie. I need you both at the main exhibit soon. Everyone else, **lock down** your sections for phase two."

"Okay, you heard her. Everyone, check your watches. Secure your areas. Make sure no one gets in or out. Guards on the outside and in the parking garage need to tell visitors that the museum is temporarily closed due to a vermin outbreak."

"You calling us rats?" someone asks. Laughter **breaks out**.

"Very funny. **Get into position**."

The channel goes quiet. Things have **taken a serious turn for the worst**. If there is a **bright side**, at least you know that the people in charge are going to be at the main exhibit.

What could they be doing there? And then it **dawns on you**: They are going to steal the *Girl with a Pearl Earring*.

You need to rescue Darla and get out of here. But how?

Suddenly, from outside the gift shop, you hear glass crunch underfoot. You **peek out** from behind the counter and see a guard. Unlike the others, though, this one looks **scared out of his wits**. He enters the gift shop slowly and **jumps** at every sound he hears. Eventually, he dashes to the counter and crashes into you. An awkward silence fills the room as you both stare at each other.

"*S'arrêter là!*" he whispers. The frantic guard points his flashlight directly into your eyes, blinding you.

"Hey!" You take your flashlight and do the same.

"*S'arrêter là!*" he repeats, whispering even louder.

"I don't speak French," you tell him.

"Quiet!" the guard hisses. "Make no sound!"

"You're the one **making all the racket!**"

You make a **mental note** that the guard speaks with a heavy French accent. It seems obvious this man has no ties with the art thieves posing as guards. Just to be sure, you feel for the fake gun in your pocket. If **worse comes to worst**, it might be the only way to make him to listen to what you have to say.

"I'm going to need your help," you say.

"Quiet!" The guard gives you an angry look and begins to wrestle you for your flashlight.

Outside the gift shop, you suddenly hear the sound of heavy footsteps coming your way The scared guard **turns off** his flashlight and reaches over with a shaky hand to cover yours.

"Please," you try again.

The guard takes the flashlight from you and shakes it at you.

"Can you please **calm down** and listen to me?"

"I will not help you," he says. "I will never help a thief!"

"I'm not a thief!"

He snorts. "Why should I believe you?"

"Listen!" you say as loudly as you can without getting the attention of whoever is **sneaking around** outside the gift shop now. At the same time, you slowly reach for the fake gun. It looks like the guard is going to **take some convincing**.

"Just **drop it**!" the guard stammers.

If you think that the guard must see the gun on you and is asking you to drop your weapon to the ground, go to **page 76**.

If you think that the guard is asking you to stop arguing with him and to surrender quietly, go to **page 89**.

"**Speak up**," the museum attendant tells you. He has a thick French accent. "Where do you think you are going, *monsieur*?"

"I'm, uh, looking for my tour group," you lie.

"This is not the way. I doubt your tour group left through this door," he says gruffly. "Please go directly to the main entrance of the museum. Service exits are off-limits, and our emergency exits are **out of service** right now."

"Kind of ironic to have emergency exits that don't work in an emergency," you quip.

"Enough!"

"But my phone!" you say. "My wallet!"

The attendant asks you to repeat what you just said. You explain how you lost your things.

"I am sorry, *monsieur*," the man says. "You will have to come back tomorrow and talk to Guest Services. They have a **lost and found**."

He seems sincere. You can tell he is just as **stressed out** as you are. But coming back to this museum is the last thing you want to do. You start arguing with him again when the alarm suddenly stops. Your voice echoes loudly in the room, which is now much emptier.

"Looks like it was a **false alarm**," you say more quietly, **caught off guard**.

"We will do an investigation. Now, you must still exit the museum," the attendant insists, **taking your arm**.

"I have **no head** for directions," you say. "**Do you mind** walking me over to Guest Services so I know where to find it tomorrow?"

The attendant looks around the gallery. Most of the visitors are gathering in the corridor now and **heading** to the main entrance. "Fine, fine," he says, sighing. "This way, *monsieur*."

As the attendant escorts you back, a fight **breaks out**. Several tourists argue with each other, **getting in each other's faces**. Before they can **exchange blows**, the attendant runs toward the quarreling group.

Here's my chance!

While he is distracted, you **give him the slip**.

In no time, you are standing in front of the service door again. You put your hand on the door, ready to open it, but you start to have **second thoughts**.

*What if I left my wallet back at the hostel or on the bus? Maybe that guy didn't steal it after all, and I'm just **freaking out** over nothing.*

The empty gallery makes you feel cold and lonely. You have already lost your friends, your wallet, and your phone—and the day isn't even **half over** yet. You look **long and hard** at the door.

You remember something Darla said to you back at the hostel when she asked you why you didn't have a girlfriend. "You are too shy," she said, touching your hand and chiding you. "Sammy, you need to be more of a **go-getter**."

If Darla's words make you want to go through the service door and find the suspect yourself, go to **page 55**.

If Darla's words make you think you should go now and get help from the Guest Services booth, go to **page 69**.

Darla is saying you should ignore her request and go with your plan to go to the museum entrance. You assume that this means you can forget her ridiculous idea to stay. You feel unsafe being stuck in one area, especially with the possibility of a fire in the building. With all of the old artwork and frames hanging around the building, you know the museum is **one bad spark away** from turning into a giant bonfire.

"Well, let's go," you tell Darla. "We can still **catch up** with the crowds that are leaving."

Darla nods and follows you out of the gallery before the gate drops to the floor and seals off the section from the hallway.

"So, that's that," Darla says, putting her hands on her hips. "We're **out in the open** with two different directions to go." She points at the far end of the room, away from the main entrance. "Past those sculptures, we can head to the East Wing, I think."

"What do you mean? That goes deeper inside the museum."

"I know," Darla says dryly. "I'm not leaving here until I know what's **going on**. Aren't you even a little bit curious about what's happening?"

"I am, but since you said the decision was **up to me**, I'm saying it's safer to go with my plan."

"I was hoping you would choose to listen to my advice and trust me. Something is definitely **off** about all of this. Don't you think it's suspicious that they're lowering the security gates? If there was truly a fire, you wouldn't **lock** people **in**."

"What do you think is happening? A terrorist attack? An art heist?" you say jokingly. The look on Darla's face makes you wonder if you **hit a nerve**.

Over Darla's shoulder, you see a red light in the corner of the room, moving side to side. It is a security camera.

"Hello! Over here!" you shout, waving your arms back and forth at the big eye in the room. "You think anyone is watching?" you ask Darla.

Darla grabs you and moves you away from it. "**Keep out of sight!**" she snaps. "Now, let me think for a minute."

"This isn't like you," you observe. "Do you know something?"

"Sammy," she says, sighing. "I think it's time I told you a secret." She exhales deeply. "I haven't been honest with you about who I am."

"What do you mean?"

"I'm an agent with Interpol."

You smile, thinking Darla's **playing a trick** on you. "Yeah, right. **Nice try**, Agent Darla."

She nods grimly. "I've been **helping out** on a case involving an art thief we can't seem to catch. She likes to target small museums, so the division hasn't put all of its resources into catching her. But it's been a **personal mission** of mine. I suspected she was going to steal this painting because it would be a **big score**, and the small museum fits her comfort zone. My suspicions were confirmed when an informant said **something big was going to happen** in Lyon."

"Interpol?" you mouth, astounded.

"Did you even hear what I just said?"

"Interpol . . ." you say again **under your breath**.

"Yes, Sammy. That's why I need you to **follow my lead** on this."

"So, this isn't about a fire?"

Darla sighs again. "No."

"We're in the **middle of** an art heist?" You can feel the blood drain from you face. You feel **lightheaded**, even a little giddy. You want to laugh.

"Yes, a heist organized by Madeleine de Castellano."

"Madeleine," you repeat.

"She also **goes by** Maddy to her associates."

"Maddy?" you gasp again. You have the sudden urge to **sit down**. "I met a Maddy earlier today while I was standing in line. We talked. Chatted really."

"What?" Darla exclaims, her expression changing. She looks eagerly at you. "What did she look like?"

You tell her about Maddy's striking features—those green eyes—and her thick black coat. "She was in the main exhibit right behind me while you and Eric were looking at the painting."

"Congratulations," Darla says, impressed. "You were **face to face** with a major criminal. That's Maddy, all right. She's becoming a real celebrity in the **criminal underground**."

"She was rather talkative," you tell Darla. "Actually, she's the one who started the conversation."

"Maybe she thought you were cute," Darla says, sounding like her old self.

You **roll your eyes**. "Anyways, I remember she seemed really interested in the painting. At least, how much it was worth. She joked the whole time that she was going to steal it."

"That's bold of her. Did she mention anything in particular?"

"No, nothing **out of the ordinary**. Aside from how she looked and what she was wearing, she seemed like a regular tourist."

In the hallway, you see two guards with flashlights in the distance. They must have seen you **on camera** and now are coming to investigate.

"We can't trust them," Darla warns you, running behind a sculpture. "We can't trust anyone."

You follow her and **crouch down** behind the pedestal. "Anyone?" you say quietly.

"You can trust me, Sammy. And I've already **made up my mind** about you," Darla says. "But who knows who's working with her and who's not?"

"How are we going to get out of here?"

"Very carefully," Darla says. "Maddy might be a small-time thief, but she's one of the smartest and quickest criminals I've ever investigated. I've studied her long enough to know that she'll be tough to stop once her plan **gets rolling**. She wants that painting very badly, and she'll **pull out all the stops** to get it."

"We should try to **call back-up**, right?"

"That's where you **come in**, Sammy."

"Me?"

"If you can get out of here and notify the authorities, I can **work on the inside** and **slow them down**."

"Then, let me talk to these guards. I'll **play dumb**. Even if they're working for Maddy, they'll just let me out."

"I can't say **for sure** that your plan will work."

"Well, someone's got to talk to them because they're obviously looking for me now," you reason. "And they'll **comb through** this area until they find me, which makes it possible they'll find you—unless we **split up**."

"Okay, that **makes sense**," Darla says, nodding.

"**Here goes nothing** then," you say. "And if we **get out of this alive**, drinks are definitely **on you**."

Darla smiles. "You've got a deal."

Taking a few steps away from the statue, you go to one of the walls. You wait a few seconds as Darla runs to the opposite end of the gallery, making sure the statues keep her out of the guards' **line of sight**.

"Hello, there," you say, approaching the guards. They shine their flashlights in your face, and you **hold up** your hands. "I need help getting out of here. I bet you guys **know your way around**."

One of the guards gets on his walkie-talkie as the other looks you up and down. You expect the guards to walk you to the museum entrance, but interestingly enough, the gates on one side of the gallery begin to rise. The guard who was on the walkie-talkie points toward the entrance.

"Isn't the exit that way?" you ask, pointing in the other direction.

The guards stare at you coldly, waiting for you to move. "Sorry, we need you to go that way," one of them says.

You decide to follow their orders and walk under the rising gate. From there, the corridor leads you into a series of smaller galleries that are all interconnected. If you can lose them here, you might be able to find a way back to the main entrance or to an emergency exit. You look over your shoulder at the guards while you quicken your pace.

"Hey, slow down!" one of them complains.

Without looking back, you **take off running** into the maze of galleries. Each room you run through looks identical to the one before. As you enter one room and then go through another, you notice that there are more benches and alcoves. Unlike in the sculpture gallery, though, there are no objects to hide behind for **cover**. If you keep running through these interconnected rooms, you will eventually **run into** one of the guards.

You listen for footsteps and enter a corner gallery with two open entrances and one service door.

It's possible they were leading me to this service door anyway. Maybe I should wait here and talk to them.

You know it is a risk. If the guards **happen to be** a part of Maddy's crew, you could **end up worse off** than before. The guards also won't be too happy that you ran away from them. You consider the service door too. You test it, pushing on it, and it easily swings opens. You quickly peek behind the door and see nothing **out of the ordinary**—just a quieter, darker exterior part of the museum. Meanwhile, the footsteps are getting louder from each direction. **Before you know it**, the guards will have you **cornered** and trapped inside the gallery.

Suddenly, you remember what Eric told you once: "If you're ever in a situation where you don't know what to do and are **faced with** two bad choices, **better the devil you know than the devil you don't know.**"

> If you decide to go through the service exit, go to **page 55**.

> If you decide to put your trust in the guards and wait for them at the door, go to **page 64**.

The guard is asking you to obey their orders without question. You decide it is best to do as they say.

Waving his gun in the direction of the staircase, the big guard tells you to continue walking up to the second floor.

"Take the girl," the smaller guard tells the larger one. "Find out who she is and whoever she's working for."

"And this one?" the big guard says, pointing to you.

"I'll do the same. We need to keep them separated. It helps us keep things organized."

Darla struggles weakly as the large guard hoists her over his shoulder. While he takes her away, the smaller guard walks you into a gallery space filled with earthenware and fine porcelain. You see a sign.

Poterie et Vases

"Right there is good," he says, stopping you in the middle of the Pottery and Vases gallery. "Now, sit," he orders. He holsters his pistol and takes out a messy coil of rope hanging from his belt. Cursing under his breath, he begins to untangle the strands. "Don't move," he warns you.

Frustrated that it is taking so long to straighten out the rope, the guard begins to whip it around violently, causing it to tangle even more. You watch in fascination as the man gets more **riled up**.

"Are you kidding me?" he exclaims, shaking the tangled rope.

Go time.

You run and lunge at his legs, knocking him back into a large vase that shatters under his weight. The guard screams as shards of clay dig into his neck and shoulders. He reaches for his gun and pulls it out of the holster. But since his hands are covered in blood and clay dust, he loses his grip.

You grab for the gun and manage to take it. You try to keep your hands from shaking as you point the pistol at him.

"I told you not to touch that," the guard tells you, **standing up**. As his hand moves to his nightstick, you point the gun up at the ceiling and pull the trigger to **scare him off**. To your surprise, all you hear is a light click.

The man laughs. "You can't shoot me, so you better—"

You swing the fake gun around and hit him in the face. It may be a fake gun, but it can still hurt.

"Son of a—!" he screams, clutching his cheek.

Before he can recover, you grab the tangled rope and toss it over him, pulling it tight around his body. He tries to **stay on his feet**, hopping to keep his balance, but you push him headfirst into a large marble statue. The man wobbles from the blow and then falls to the floor in a heap.

You stare down at the man's prone body and wonder at how you managed to do it. "Not good, not good," you keep muttering to yourself. The adrenaline still pumping through your veins makes you jumpy.

You can't **take any chances** that he will **come to**. Taking his belt, you **tie him up**, binding his wrists. Before you leave, you take his fake gun, nightstick, and flashlight. Digging through the guard's pockets, you also find a walkie-talkie.

Up ahead, security gates have come down. In the remaining open areas, rows of glass cases and walled sections keep you out of direct **line of sight**, but nothing provides a perfect **cover**. You keep walking and notice another sign.

Tapisseries

The Tapestries gallery. Filled with embroidered and woven fabrics hanging from the ceiling or draped over the walls, the room could be a good **hiding spot** while you **take stock** of your situation.

As you walk toward the gallery, the walkie-talkie vibrates in your hand. You hold it to your ear.

"Status report," a voice demands.

"All clear here at the main entrance. The last tourist left a few minutes ago, and we just **finished a sweep** and found no one else."

"All clear here in the office and storerooms," another voice chimes in. "Museum staffers are gone, and the hostages are secure."

"East Wing?"

"Barrett here. Problem in the East Wing. Found a couple here. I'm questioning the woman now," the man responds. You recognize the Australian accent.

"Fine. Get what you need. As soon as you're finished, I need you at the main exhibit. The rest of you, get ready for phase two."

These guards are obviously **up to something**. You know that Darla is somewhere on the roof with the big guard. There isn't much you can do **all by yourself**. You need to find a way to **get the upper hand**.

Suddenly, another voice gets on the walkie-talkie.

"This is Willie. I've just been attacked. East Wing is not clear. Repeat. East Wing. Not clear."

The channel goes quiet, and you feel a **cold chill rush down your spine**. You can't save Darla yet, not until you deal with Willie. You will also have to avoid anyone else who will be **on the lookout** for you. Should you **stay put** and wait **in hiding**? The tapestries offer good shelter, but you realize that the thieves are smarter than they look and will probably check obvious hiding spots like this one.

Then, across the gallery floor, you see a sign.

Toilettes

The bathrooms. It could either be a safe place to **lie low** and hide or a place to get trapped and caught. Holding the walkie-talkie to your ear, you wait for someone to speak. Over the next few minutes, only random chatter comes through. All of a sudden, you hear the voice of someone that surprises you.

"Barrett," a woman speaks. Her voice is familiar.

"Barrett here," the man answers. "Go ahead, Madeleine."

Madeleine?

"How much more time until you're ready?"

"I'm a little busy at the moment. Found another tourist wandering through the offices. I'll make sure he's **put away**."

"Get another group on it. I need you here. Main exhibit. Now."

All of a sudden, another voice screams over the radio. "I'm **on to you**, guys. I'm going to make sure you don't get out of here with that painting! Bwah!"

The sudden loudness of the voice startles you until you realize you recognize it.

"Who was that?" Madeleine asks.

"You'll know who I am when you read it in the paper," the familiar voice says. "I'm **taking you all down**! Bwah!"

What the . . . Eric?

You hesitate for a second before you press the talk button on the walkie-talkie. "Um, Sanders?" you say, calling Eric by his last name.

"So. You must have heard of me," Eric says defiantly.

The walkie-talkie buzzes in your hand as various voices begin to talk all at once.

"Find those idiots and **clear this channel**," an angry Madeleine orders.

You are **faced with** a tough choice. You can either keep looking for Darla or head to the offices and help Eric.

>If you decide to go downstairs and look for Eric, go to **page 184**.

>If you decide to keep looking for Darla, go to **page 207**.

[CHAPTER TWO]

~Down the Rabbit Hole

YOU WALK THROUGH the service door. It opens quietly, and you are immediately blinded by bright sunlight. "**Down the rabbit hole**," you say to yourself. When your eyes adjust, you **look around** at an alleyway behind the museum that connects the main building to a smaller structure, probably a utility building or storage section. The paved alleyway is long and flanked on both sides by tall walls. At the far end of the path, a group of guards stands huddled in front of a door to the other building.

You think about approaching the group but hesitate. They haven't noticed you yet; they seem concentrated on getting the door to the other building open. You take slow, careful steps, keeping as quiet as possible. The guards are preoccupied, opening their duffel bags and removing their jackets and caps. They don't seem to hear you walking in their direction. Underneath their uniforms, the guards wear padded shirts. Walkie-talkies buzz, and a few of the guards **take out** tools from the duffel bags. One of them walks to the door with a blowtorch in hand.

When two of the men start to shout and push each other, you freeze mid-step. Before they look up and see you, you slide behind a dumpster located near the wall. The men don't **spot you**, and you hope that you stay unnoticed—a **fly on the wall**.

"Are you serious?" one of them yells, his voice echoing through the alley. "Do I need to **bash your brains in**?"

"I just really want to know. What if something goes wrong? What if the other security guards decide to fight back?"

"Look, Jacques, since you're a newbie, I'll humor you and answer your question. Then you're going to have to **shut up** already."

"First of all, my name isn't Jacques, Barrett. My name is Francois. Okay?"

"Do I look like I care?" Barrett says. "You're here to follow my orders. If I want to call you Jacques, then that's what I'm calling you."

A calming voice interrupts. "Enough already. **Set your watches** because we're going to the next phase of this operation in exactly thirty minutes. That **leaves us** about ten minutes to cut the power. But first we need to get through this door."

"Listen to Harry," Barrett says.

"And the security guards on our side?" Francois asks. "How do we know they'll **come through** and capture the other ones?"

"Because we trust them," Barrett says, trying to control his anger.

"He's right," Harry says. "Without trust, this whole thing **falls apart**."

"I am not the kind of guy who **leaves anything to chance**," Francois says, obviously unhappy with the answer. "I want to be sure everything is just right."

"Not leaving anything to chance is the motto of this group," another male voice chimes in. "You and the guards we've **paid off** outnumber the guards on duty who have no idea what's happening. They **won't know what hit them**."

"See, Jacques?" Barrett says mockingly. "**This isn't our first rodeo**. You need to stop questioning the plan. We've done this before—and it won't be our last. Even Interpol can't **figure out** how to stop us."

Suddenly, a woman interrupts the squabble. Her voice **cuts through the noise**. "**Get it together**, or else I'll slice you both open and leave you in that dumpster."

You crane your neck to get a better look and watch as the woman **takes off** her thick black coat. Her back is toward you. She **hikes up her dress** and reveals a switchblade strapped to her thigh.

"Francois," she continues. "You want to know how we can trust this team? This is why."

The woman takes the switchblade and holds the handle dangerously close to his cheek. You hear the sound of a blade quickly unfolding from its handle. Francois gasps. The rest of the men laugh as Francois **turns bright red** and nearly faints.

The woman kneels down and begins to cut away at the edges of her coat on the ground. She does the same to the other jackets and removes the lining from each. One by one, the guards take turns **picking up** items hidden inside the panels. One man **pulls out** a set of weapons, **handing them out**. You see crowbars and other tools.

"Who wants to steal a painting?" Barrett asks, rallying the group.

The men cheer while the woman walks silently to the opposite side and **lights up** a cigarette. As the men **go to work** getting the door open, the woman **leans back** against the wall, the smoke from her cigarette lingering in the cold morning air around her face. When the woman finishes her cigarette, she waves her hand and blows the smoke away. When you finally see her face, you feel your **blood run cold**.

Maddy.

Your legs go weak, and you feel like you are about to **tip over** and **pass out**. Your hand reaches out to steady yourself, and you hit the dumpster with a loud *clang*.

The group goes completely silent. You wish you could get a better look at their reaction, but all you can do is cower in your hiding place and wait. Your eyes **zero-in** on the service door you came through. If you were to run for it, could you reach it **in time**?

You can hear the sound of gravel crunching underfoot. The men are walking in your direction. You do everything you can to control your breathing. **Time is running out.**

"Where you guys going?"

"We heard something."

"Probably just rats."

"Can't be too sure. What if it's a rat who's gonna **rat us out**?"

"Hah. Aren't you the comedian."

Maddy shouts over them to get their attention. You risk another peek at the group. The men turn to watch Maddy expectantly, like a **pack of dogs** she has perfectly trained. There is a long pause before she quietly gives them an order: "Whatever or whoever it is, **take care of it.**"

If you think that Maddy has ordered her men to harm whomever they find, go to **page 59**.

If you think that Maddy has ordered her men to protect whomever they find, go to **page 87**.

Maddy has ordered her men to harm whomever they find. "**Take care of it**," Maddy repeats. There is a loud *clang* as the heavy metal locks on the door fall to the ground. "We have more important things to attend to."

You listen as the *click-clack* of her high heels disappears through the open door. From the sound of her voice, you decide it will probably be best if you run now, but your body refuses to respond. You stay **frozen in place**. The men are walking toward you now, their footsteps getting louder and frighteningly close. You shift your legs into a running stance and put your hands on the ground. You close your eyes **for a second** and then launch yourself forward.

Time seems to **slow to a crawl**. The distance between you and the service door back to the museum seems like a mile away. Your hand reaches out for the door handle just as you hear feet shuffle behind you. You touch the cold metal handle of the door for a moment before the feeling is **ripped away**. Someone grabs your shirt collar and yanks you back.

Before you know it, you have **hit the pavement**. You are now **flat on your back** with the **wind knocked out of you**.

Someone kneels over you. The glint from a knife's blade shines in your eye.

"What are you doing, Frankie?" one of his colleagues ask.

"**Taking out the trash**. What does it look like I'm doing?" Frankie responds. He brings his face closer to yours, and you recognize the man as the guard who **bumped into you** earlier.

The other guard pulls him away from you. "**Cool your jets**. That's not how we do things around here," he says. "Let's **figure out** how to do this the **clean way**."

"It's how we *should* be doing things," Frankie says, shaking his head in disgust. He turns back to you. "Who are you?" he demands. "What were you doing out here?"

Before you can answer, Frankie kicks you in the ribs with his boot. You cough and groan in pain.

"Frankie! **Easy does it!**" the other guard says.

You try to **roll away**, but the heavyset guard puts his knee in your back. "Don't move, or I swear I will sink this knife so deep inside you the doctor will need a diving suit to come **fish it out**. You hear me?"

You nod emphatically.

"And you, *Tobin*!" he says, shouting at his associate with scorn in his voice. "If you say my name again today, it will be the last thing you ever say."

"We need to find a way to make sure this doesn't **come back and bite us**. Killing him will just **screw up** this whole operation and piss off Maddy."

"What are you suggesting?"

Tobin points to the dumpster. "You said something about **taking out the trash**, didn't you?"

Frankie grunts, considering the idea. Then his hands go under your armpits, and he lifts you **to your feet**. Your ribs are **on fire**. You struggle and try to **fight him off**, but you only manage to hurt yourself. Before you can protest further, Frankie and Tobin toss you inside the dumpster, shut the lid, and slide the latch into place.

"You better hope that **holds**," Frankie says to Tobin. "For your sake."

Counting the minutes in your head, you wait until you can't hear any more footsteps. When you think you are finally alone, you **push up** on the dumpster lid, testing the resistance. The latch jiggles in place. If only there were something thin enough to slide under the lid and long enough to reach the hook on the latch.

Your hands move slowly, feeling around in the dark. You blindly tear open a few trash bags and dig through their contents. The smell is overwhelming, but you manage to **hold back** from **throwing up**. One of the torn bags spills some hard objects onto the metal floor. **Picking up** one of them, you inspect it in the dim light. It appears to be a broken piece from a wood frame shaped like an L.

You hold the short end and stick the longer end through a gap in the lid. You aim for the metal latch, sliding the wood piece side to side until you finally dislodge the latch. You put your hands under the lid and push. The fresh air you breathe when the dumpster lid opens almost makes you cry.

The same time you kick your leg over the side, the service door starts to open. You quickly crouch back down inside the dumpster.

"You sure about this?" a male voice with a French accent asks.

"It's just a quick **smoke break**. I need some air. I'm getting hot in this uniform," another male voice says, noticeably with no accent. "How do you **stand** wearing them?"

"You get used to it."

You hear the unmistakable sound of a pack of cigarettes hitting someone's palm.

"I've been meaning to ask. How long have you worked as a security guard here?"

"For a while. I used to be a real policeman, you know? But things didn't **work out**. It didn't **suit** my—how do you say in English—personality," the French security guard says.

"Babysitting old artwork suits it better?" The other guard laughs and **takes a long drag** from his cigarette.

"No, but it **pays the bills** for now," the ex-cop responds.

"Why did you quit the police force?"

"I wasn't afraid to **get my hands dirty**, if you know what I mean."

> If you think that the security guard is saying he is a hard worker and trustworthy enough to tell about the events you just witnessed, go to **page 62**.
>
> If you think that the ex-cop is admitting he is corrupt, and you shouldn't trust him, go to **page 82**.

The security guard is saying he is a hard worker and trustworthy enough to tell about the events you just witnessed. Since the ex-cop has a history of **getting his hands dirty**, you assume he might be inclined to help you get out of this mess.

You **pop your head out** from your hiding spot. "Help!" you shout, revealing yourself to the surprised guards. "Some guys threw me in this dumpster. They went that way!" You point down the alley to the busted door.

The two guards **exchange looks** before they come alongside you and pull you out of the trash. They watch you silently as you **straighten yourself out**, brushing away garbage and debris from your clothes.

"I'm so glad you guys came," you say.

"Who threw you inside the dumpster?" the ex-cop asks, handing you a napkin.

You start to answer but then remember what Francois said a few minutes ago: "*And the security guards on our side? How do we know they'll come through and capture the other ones?*"

You wonder if you can trust these museum guards. Are they like Francois—guards **working in the pocket of** the art thieves?

"Um, it's sort of a long story," you tell the ex-cop with some hesitation. You start to doubt your decision to **pin your hopes on** these guards. "I came through that service exit a while ago, and I, uh, saw a group of people over that way. They looked **kind of shady**, but I didn't know what they were doing."

The guards' walkie-talkies squeak.

"You saw a group of people over there?" the ex-cop asks, pointing to the door at the end of the alley. "And they looked suspicious?"

"They had tools with them. Blowtorch. Crowbars."

"Tools?" The ex-cop **seems a little lost** as he talks to you, as if he has no idea what to do next.

The other guard, meanwhile, has walked away to talk to

someone on his walkie-talkie. He turns to the ex-cop and asks, "**What's the story** on this one?"

"I need you to tell us everything that you saw here," the ex-cop tells you.

Judging by the expression on his face and the way he leans in to listen to you, he seems very interested in what you have to say. You look back at the other guard who **eyes you** suspiciously as he continues his conversation on the walkie-talkie.

"I, uh, came through that door," you say, pointing back at the service door. "I saw some men over at that end. I'm not saying I know what's happening here. Hey, I'm in a **tight spot**. I just want to get out of here." You spread your arms, displaying your dirtied clothes.

"Are you a visitor to the museum?" the ex-cop asks.

"Uh, *yes*," you respond with a **bit of attitude**. "I came here with some friends. Can't you tell I'm a tourist?"

"One moment," the guy on the walkie-talkie says. He walks toward the other guard. The two whisper to each other.

"Can you help?" you ask when they turn back to you.

"*Oui*. We can help you find your friends," the ex-cop says.

Go to **page 64.**

"Follow us," the guards say, grabbing you by the arm and leading you back the way you came.

You follow the pair of guards through the empty museum. The galleries are now eerily spooky under the dim lights. There is **no sign** of anyone as you are led into the administrative section of the museum.

"Where are we going?" you ask, looking around at the offices and cubicles. The guards ignore you.

They stop in front of a door that opens to reveal a storage closet for janitorial supplies. You manage one quick glance at one of the guards before he roughly shoves you inside and slams the door in your face. You grab a hold of the door just as a deadbolt **slides into place**, locking you inside.

"What are you doing?" you shout, pounding on the door with your fists. "Let me out!" You push against the door with your shoulder, but it won't budge.

Your hands frantically feel along the wall for a light switch. The overhead light **turns on** with a buzz. You look around the small room to find bottles of cleaning fluid, a few brooms and mops, and toilet paper rolls stacked neatly on the shelves. None of it seems very useful at the moment, though the broomstick might make for a makeshift weapon in case the guards return.

While you test the broomstick's sturdiness, you hear the deadbolt slide. The door **swings open**, and another person is thrown into the closet with you. You recognize your friend instantly.

"Eric!" you shout.

Eric barely notices you as he kicks at the locked door. "Had enough, eh?" he taunts, shaking the door handle.

"Eric!" you shout again, pulling him away from the door. "I've been looking for you. Where have you been?"

Eric's eyes **grow wide** when he sees you. "Sammy!" He grabs you by the shoulders and embraces you. "I fell asleep on a bench. Slept through the whole evacuation. I had my headphones on and didn't hear a thing. Next thing I know, some security guard is yelling at me in French while his buddy keeps asking me where my girlfriend is. It quickly turned into a brawl—"

"Girlfriend?"

Eric shrugs and puts his hands in his pockets. "Probably talking about Darla. We were together until I decided to **take a nap**."

"But why would they—"

"Sammy, it's amazing," Eric gushes. "Darla and I are getting closer, you know what I mean? I put my head on her shoulder when we were in line. We were talking and—"

"No," you say, annoyed that Eric's friendship with Darla has been growing. "I mean, why would they be looking for Darla?"

Eric throws up his hands. "I don't know. All I know is, I **woke up** in an empty museum, and now I'm locked in a storage closet with you." Eric smiles and puts his hand on your shoulder. "I guess it can't get any worse, right?" He chuckles to himself and starts to wander around the small space. "It's cozy in here. **No offense**, Sammy, but I wish I were locked in here with Darla right about now."

You hit Eric with the end of the broomstick.

"Hey! I was just joking. Don't **get so touchy**. Can we get out of here already? Also, where have *you* been?"

Eric grabs the broomstick away from you and swings it like a sword while you think of an answer. "Getting left behind," you say bitterly. "You and Darla succeeded in ditching your **third wheel**."

"We definitely didn't mean to leave you behind like that. But can you blame me? Darla is so hot! I couldn't waste the chance."

You **roll your eyes**. "This was supposed to be our trip. Remember? If I knew it was the 'Eric Dates Women All Over Europe Tour,' I would have just stayed home."

Eric drops his head. "Yeah, I'm sorry, buddy. I know how hard it is for you to **come out of your shell**. Admit it, though: You've been having a lot of fun, right?"

You shake your head. Now isn't the time to start a conversation about your social anxieties. "I was until today," you say, though a part of you is rather enjoying this. Even with your bruised ribs.

A dull boom from outside rattles the walls. The closet light **blinks on and off**.

"That's our **cue**," Eric says, **cracking his knuckles**.

You hear the sound of rustling followed by the familiar jingle of keys. "What are you doing?" you ask.

"Getting us out of here," Eric responds.

One by one, Eric inserts each of the keys, trying to unlock the door. "A door with double locks. Crazy, right?" He jiggles the keys. "Come on," he urges. Finally, one of the keys turns the lock.

The door **swings open**. Outside, the hallway is dark, lit only by a few emergency lights.

"Where did you find the keys?"

"One of the guards looked like he wanted to fight, so I let him come at me. I took these out of his pocket when we were grappling on the ground. I knew they would **come in handy**."

"You fought and pickpocketed a guard?"

"Sort of. It wasn't a very fair fight. For him."

You slap your forehead. "Um, and what happens when he realizes his keys are gone?"

Eric points outside. "We'll be **long gone** before he comes back here."

Carefully, your friend checks the hallway to make sure the **coast is clear**. Dropping to the ground, he **crawls on his hands and knees** to a set of cubicles where he **pulls out** a rolling chair from one of the desks. He **ducks** underneath and motions for you to join him. The carpet is rough. Crawling on the floor scrapes your knees. As you squeeze under the desk alongside Eric, he slides the chair back into place, concealing the both of you. It is a good hiding spot for now, except you have no clear view of anything.

"Everyone's gone," Eric whispers.

"The evacuation **came out of nowhere**. A fire maybe?"

"Why would they **lock up** people if there was a fire? Plus, the place would be **crawling with** firefighters by now."

"Yeah, who locks people in at all?" you ask. "It's like we were in museum jail."

Eric **crosses his arms** and hums to himself. "Okay, let's **think this through**," he says. "Fire alarms, lights flickering off and on, guards **beating up** on visitors, guards **locking up** visitors. Strange. An empty museum. And a world-famous painting on exhibit." He snaps his fingers. "That could only **add up** to one thing."

"What?"

"This might sound a bit crazy," Eric says, "but I think we're in the middle of an art heist."

You scoff. "That's your theory? From all that, you get criminals are here to steal the *Girl with a Pearl Earring*?"

Eric grins. "Wouldn't it be awesome?"

You groan. Having known Eric for as long as you have, he has always had a reputation for **jumping to conclusions** and **talking a big game**. "Eric, even if that were happening, I wouldn't say it would be awesome."

"Do you doubt my detective skills? **Run with it**. Fire alarms. Empty museum. Guards taking and locking tourists in closets. Don't forget—famous painting. Do I have to say it again? Famous. Painting. What else would convince you?"

"It's not the convincing part," you object. "I just don't want to believe it. Let's just get out of here as soon as possible."

Eric stares in disbelief. "And miss all the fun?"

"Fun?" you stammer. "How is any of this fun?"

"Because we have **front row seats**," Eric explains. "Because we can be heroes."

"Whoa!" you exclaim. "Let me stop you right there."

"Can't stop this!" Eric says, beating on his chest. "You and me, together, against a bunch of thieves. Like Batman and Robin."

"Um, we are not Batman—"

Eric lowers his voice and says, "No, we are not. *I* am Batman, and *you* are Robin."

"But Batman is *my* favorite character." You start to laugh. "Can we please focus on getting out of here?" You check your pockets for your map of the museum.

"Well, I **happen to know** the way out of here," Eric says in his Batman voice. "A few doors back that way goes into the Main Hall," he says, pointing to a door at the opposite end of the room.

You both crawl out from under the desk. At the door, Eric stops and turns to you. "I just want to do one thing," he says.

You sigh and **put away** your map. "What now?"

"I want to prove to you that there *is* an art heist happening **right under our noses**."

"All you're proving is that you're an idiot!"

"Help me, Sammy," Eric says, his eyes glinting with excitement. "We can **take down** these guys. Do it for the museum! Do it for France! Do it for the girl wearing that earring!"

You know that once Eric has his **mind set on something**, it is almost impossible to get him to **listen to reason**. If you refuse to help him, he will insist on doing this on his own.

"Fine. But I'm doing this for you. Not for some **flight of fancy**."

He cheers. "We can do this, Sammy." Eric laughs, sounding like a madman. "The two of us can **even out the odds**."

If you think that Eric means that working together as a team will help you deal with the art thieves, go to **page 106**.

If you think that Eric's math is wrong—there are only two of you against a whole gang of criminals—and you think you need to find more help, go to **page 155**.

You think about your options and what you can do to **fix things**, and you decide to go to the Guest Services booth. You immediately regret your choice. You wonder if you just lost your one and only chance to find the person who may have taken your stuff. At one point, someone bumps into you again, and you find yourself thinking cynical thoughts.

Hah! Hate to disappoint you, but someone already took everything I have.

Feeling a little emotional and raw, you force yourself to **take a mental step back**. As angry and frustrated as you are, you know you have to get through the day without **lashing out** at others.

Up ahead, you see the Guest Services booth tended by an older gentleman. He greets you **on sight** with a big smile and a salute. Short in stature and dressed in tweed, tufts of white hair behind his ears, the man reminds you of your grandfather.

"*Puis-je vous aider*? How can I help you?" he asks cheerfully.

"I just lost my wallet and phone."

"A tragedy, *monsieur*!" he exclaims. "How can we help?"

"I was hoping you'd have some ideas."

The gentleman begins shuffling through a stack of papers. He grabs a sheet and slides the paper toward you.

"What is this?" you ask, annoyed that the document is in French.

"It is a **lost and found** ticket," he tells you.

You sigh, staring at the words in French.

The attendant clasps his hands together. "I will help you," he says gently. "After you **fill out** this form, if your belongings appear, we will call you," he says. "Name. Phone number, if you have. Description of lost item." The attendant points at each of the boxes in **rapid-fire** mode.

Inwardly, you groan. You regret coming to the booth. Maybe you should just **give up** on your things. **Filling out** paperwork won't help. You should have been more proactive about finding your things on your own. You think bitterly about the man who bumped into you.

"I know the **chances are slim**," the elderly gentleman says, noticing how upset you are. "Hopefully, your property will **turn up**. Do not lose faith. There are honest people out there."

You force yourself to thank the worker politely. *It's not his fault.*

Around the desk, you notice security monitors featuring screens that show various room and galleries in the museum. Squinting your eyes, you recognize a sleeping figure on one of the museum benches.

Eric?

"Excuse me. Where is that?" you ask, pointing at the screen.

"That is one of the medieval arts galleries."

"Can you tell me the fastest way to get there?"

The man shows you a map. He twirls his finger in the air and then drops it down onto the sheet. "You are here," he says. His finger rises back up and twirls before dropping again. "And you want to go here." His finger lands in a section on the west side of the museum. The attendant draws a line between the two points. "You. Here. You. There."

"Got it," you say.

You **elbow your way** through the dense crowds. All the while, the lights overhead begin to flicker on and off. Once in a while, you hear a shrill blast from the fire alarms, which only **spurs** you to move faster. Is the museum having an issue with its alarm system?

What a shame—and on the first day of a special exhibition too. The museum officials must be frantic.

Suddenly, the lights **go out** altogether. You stop running, waiting for the lights to come back on, but the fire alarms keep blasting away.

Could there be a real fire?

You stop running and wait, thinking the alarms will **turn off**. When the lights finally return, you notice they are much dimmer than before.

Over the loud blasts from the alarms, museum officials shout, ordering people to leave the museum immediately. Groups of people cram themselves into the central corridor that goes back to the Main Hall. You look in the other direction, toward the West Wing. Now you have to **fight the crowds** going the opposite way. If only you could get closer to the medieval exhibits, you might be able to see Eric as he exits into the Main Hall.

Around you, security gates begin dropping down, blocking the entryways to the various galleries. You furiously shove your away against the waves of people, **keeping an eye out** for Eric along the way. After a few minutes, the hall empties.

You think you are finally alone when a security guard confronts you. "*Pourquoi n'avez-vous pas quitté le musée?*" he says, rushing to your side.

"Sorry, I don't speak French," you tell him.

"Hello!" he says, **starting over**. "*Monsieur*, why are you not leaving the museum? There is an evacuation. You cannot be here."

"I'm looking for a friend. He fell asleep on a bench."

Without **taking his eyes off of you**, the guard **pulls out** his walkie-talkie. "*J'ai trouvé une vistor. Que dois-je faire,*" he says.

You try to walk away, but the guard grabs your arm.

"Please wait," he says.

After a few seconds, another guard arrives, and the two of them speak to each other for a moment.

"You are looking for your friend, *oui*?" the second guard asks.

"Yes," you reply. "I think he might have **dozed off** somewhere."

The man **snaps his fingers**. "Ah! We will take you to him."

"But you don't even know who he is," you interject.

You wonder if it is a language problem. *Am I not **making myself clear**?*

"We will take you to him," the guard repeats confidently.

Go to **page 64**.

The tourist is commenting on how you fell hard on the ground when the man ran into you.

You stare stonily at the gawking visitor. "You don't have to be jerk about it."

"Hey, man, it's not me you should be angry at. That guy is **getting away** with your things." He points in the far distance. "You've been **taken for a ride**," he repeats.

You silently pat your pockets. *Oh. I guess I have* . . .

The tourist wasn't **making fun of you**. He was **pointing out** how the man who bumped into you **ripped you off** and stole your things.

You mumble a curt apology.

Go to **page 69.**

Finally!

At last, something interesting is happening in the museum. Maybe the day won't **end on a bad note** after all.

"What's going on?" you ask Darla when you **catch up** to her.

"I have a feeling things are going to get worse before they get any better," Darla says. "It might be best if you left the museum, Sammy. I can't say why right now, but you have to trust me." She touches your hand and leans in closer. "**Don't get me wrong**. I'm thankful you want to stay with me."

Before you can respond, Darla snatches her purse from you and disappears deeper into the museum.

The gallery lights flicker and then go dark. The crowd gasps before settling into a tense moment of silence. Eventually, the emergency lights are **tripped**. They cast an eerie glow around you. Over the whispers of the crowd, the fire alarms blare much louder than before.

Even in the dim light, you can still see Darla up ahead. Your instincts tell you to go after her. Security guards and museum attendants direct everyone to the main entrance, making it harder for you to push through in the opposite direction. One of the museum attendants points at you and orders you to turn around and follow the crowd, but you ignore him.

"Stop!" you shout at Darla as you **swim against the tide** of people.

Darla yells something over the alarm. She trips and falls to the ground, almost crushed, as panicked museum visitors begin to push and shove each other around her. To your relief, she manages to **get back on her feet**.

While the evacuation continues, you manage to **slip out** of the forward-moving crowd and return to the sculpture room where the mysterious group of guards left in a hurry a while ago. If your **memory serves you correctly**, this part of the museum leads to the East Wing.

Screams can be heard from the previous room, but you continue on until you reach the next gallery, a large rotunda covered by a beautiful dome. Daylight falls through the skylights onto a large bronze statue of a man riding on a horse.

Walking around the bronze statue, you discover Darla sitting on the floor at the base of the pedestal.

"Just **catching my breath**," she says when she sees you. "So, you decided to stay and **crash the party**."

You nod. The alarms suddenly **cut out**, and you can speak normally again. "Which way do we go now?" you ask, looking around.

In one direction, a corridor leads further into the East Wing. In another direction, at the far side of the rotunda, a set of stairs leads up to the second floor where a photography exhibit sits behind glass doors.

"I don't know," Darla says, thinking. "Let's **split up**. I'll keep looking around the East Wing, while you go up the stairs. But don't leave the area." She emphasizes the last sentence by squeezing your shoulder before rushing past the statue and toward the corridor.

You **walk up** the steps to the second floor and approach the glass doors. They open to a gallery full of photographs.

Photographie

Behind you, you hear footsteps and freeze.

"The hallway is clear," Darla calls out. She joins you at the glass doors. "What about here?"

"Except for you, haven't heard or seen anyone," you tell her. "Not yet anyway."

"You know what's strange, though?" Darla says. "None of the emergency exits are open along the way. They're all locked. Why would they be locked? It would be against building code. A museum like this, even if it is small, wouldn't be in violation—not on a **big**

day like this. For the *Girl with a Pearl Earring*, they would make sure everything was **tip-top**."

"That is strange," you agree.

"Also, there's no cell signal anywhere," Darla says, waving her phone.

"Maybe we should **head back**," you suggest as you go back down to the main floor. You **take a second** to look around. The immense rotunda is empty and still. Though you aren't **crazy about** crowded spaces and large groups of people, you find the eerie quiet in the spacious gallery no better. In fact, it feels even more unsettling, like **the calm before the storm**.

"I don't want to **retrace our steps** just yet," Darla says. "We need to know what's happening." Her face looks fixed and determined. "Even if it means **getting our fingers burnt**."

"I'll tell you one thing," you say, uncomfortably aware how your **voice carries** in the big, empty room. "I have a **gut feeling** that this isn't about a fire."

"If you're waiting for the fire department, **don't hold your breath**."

If you think that Darla is giving you advice on how to survive a fire, go to **page 14**.

If you think that Darla believes something other than a fire is happening in the museum, go to **page 33**.

The guard must see the gun on you and is asking you to drop your weapon to the ground. You **pull it out** and brandish it in the air. "Don't worry, it's not—"

The guard is **beside himself**. "Please, please!" he says. "Do not kill me."

"You don't understand . . ." you try to explain, but the guard just **backs away** in fright. His flashlight shakes and rattles in his hand.

You lower the gun and realize he has no idea the weapon is fake. The poor man is just someone who got **caught in the wrong place at the wrong time**. He is harmless and as confused as you are about what is happening in the museum.

Before you can **calm him down**, the flashlight drops out of his hand and smacks the ground, **giving away** your hiding spot.

"Who's there?" the intruder asks. The person enters the gift shop.

The scared guard stands and **turns on his heels**, running out of the shop. You hear him bump into the intruder, who grunts and **takes off** after him.

You sigh. *It's too late for him, but I still need to be careful.*

You count to ten and wait. Except for your breathing, it is silent in the gift shop. You assume the intruder must have been alone. Slowly, you crawl out from behind the counter. The walkie-talkie at your side buzzes, and you put it to your ear.

"In pursuit, in pursuit. I'm **chasing down** a spare guard," a breathless voice states. "Looks like someone missed one."

"We're actually missing a few," another voice says.

"Messy. This makes me nervous."

"Quit whining. It's a **bump in the road**. Things like this **come with the territory**. We need to stay calm, people. Things are progressing. These guards are harmless. Most of them are just **scared out of their wits**."

"Museum's empty at the main entrance now. **Holding position**," another person reports.

"We're **tidying up** the office and storage areas."

"Okay. Everyone **do one more sweep** and make absolutely sure you have all the guards who aren't on our payroll in custody. Stay focused, or else there'll be the **devil to pay** with you-know-who."

"**Roger that**."

"Team One is starting the extraction on the package."

Team One? Extraction?

Go to **page 193**.

Tobin is planning on alerting the boss, Maddy, about Frankie to tell her what happened. Not good. More people might come, and you would be sure to be discovered then.

You **peek out** from under the desk at Tobin. He has crawled to the opposite side of the room. You watch him wipe the blood from his nose with his sleeve before he grabs a handkerchief from his pocket. His back to you, he **kneels down** and begins to wipe the concrete floor.

You have the **element of surprise on your side**. Balling your hands into fists, you run out from behind the desk. Teary-eyed Tobin is **caught off guard** by your **sneak attack**. He tumbles to the floor, and his head hits the ground. In just a few seconds, it is over. You stare in wonder at his unconscious body. Tobin is **down for the count**. The fight has ended before it even began.

"Tobin?" you check, lifting his hand and letting it drop. You say his name several times until you are confident he **poses no threat** to you. You are giddy with relief. **For good measure**, you give Tobin a light nudge in the ribs with your foot. Still, nothing.

Your eyes go to the mysterious service tunnel hatch by the desk. You wonder what you might find down there and peer into the dark hole that goes underground. You stifle the urge to shout hello into space.

Looking back at Tobin lying on the ground, you know you will have to decide what to do with him. If he tells Frankie about your escape from the dumpster, the guards will **double their efforts** to **hunt you down**.

You need to leave now. But where do you go? The hatch is a tempting option, and you could **take your chances** and go inside it, but you aren't even sure **where it leads**. What if it goes nowhere? What if it takes you right to other guards or Maddy's henchmen? Wouldn't that be the first place they would check anyway? Then there is the parking garage. But Frankie is prowling around there, and you aren't sure whether you can dodge him if he catches you.

Either way, you can't stay here and be a **sitting duck**. You have to **keep moving**, no matter which route you take.

Something on the floor **catches your eye**. Did Tobin's foot just twitch? You **inch closer** to Tobin's unconscious form and hope your **eyes are playing tricks on you**. Tobin's foot moves again, **dashing your hopes**. It looks like Tobin is beginning to **wake up**.

You creep away as he starts to moan and touch his head. Then his eyes open. He sees you backing away.

"Come back," Tobin says weakly. "Help me. Please."

In a **snap decision**, you go for the hatch. Peering inside, you see a ladder. You begin descending down the rungs when you hear Tobin groan again. For a second, you hesitate and consider going to his aid, but then you decide it is too risky. You check if Tobin is **coming for you**, but he is still on his knees, sweeping the floor with his hands.

"Where are my glasses?" Tobin mutters.

You **spot** his glasses on the floor. One lens is cracked, but it is otherwise intact. You quietly crawl out of the hatch and **pick up** the frames. Tobin hears your shuffling and jerks as you come near him. You wave your hand in front of his face.

"Promise me you won't try to contact your boss," you say.

"What?" Tobin says, squinting his eyes at you. "Why would I do that? Maddy can't be bothered with this. This is between me and Frankie."

You realize that Tobin wasn't thinking about calling for help or informing Maddy. "*Show him who's boss . . .* " Tobin was thinking about **getting back at** Frankie. Feeling sorry for him, you carefully put the glasses in his outstretched hand.

"Thanks, man," he says, tapping cautiously on the broken lens. "Could be worse, I guess." He **looks up** at you with a tired look of defeat.

"Listen, I don't want to fight you," you tell him.

"Are you sure about that?" Tobin asks. "Because you **knocking me out** earlier doesn't really make me want to trust you."

You **hold up** your hands in a peaceful gesture. "Well, actually, I **barely laid a finger—**" You stop when you see Tobin's face **turn red**. "Sorry about that. Look, I don't want to fight. I just want to get out of here."

Tobin **stares off into space**, and his tense body relaxes. "You're probably mad about the dumpster," he says. "I would be too. But I couldn't let him kill you. I'm not like the others."

"Thanks," you say, shrugging. "I guess."

"**Don't mention it**. Though, if they **find out** you've escaped, I won't be around much longer. These people don't look kindly on mistakes. It's not going to be just a **slap on the wrist** for me. Frankie will finally **blow his top**."

By the look on his face, you know that Tobin is telling the truth. You **swallow hard**. Does this mean he will try to recapture you to fix his mistakes? You eye him with caution and step back uneasily.

"Relax," Tobin says, holding up his hands. "I won't try to stop you. You're free to go."

"What about Frankie?"

"Either I **stand up** to him or get **beat up** again. Or worse. There's nothing I can do."

"Do you know where he is right now?" you ask.

"Probably in the parking garage loading some of the cars."

"Anyone else?"

"Guards. About three or four of them scattered throughout. There will be two at the parking garage entrance to keep visitors from entering."

"What do I do now?" you ask out loud, looking at the hatch and then back at Tobin.

"If I could suggest something . . ." Tobin starts to say.

"Yeah?"

"Ah, forget it. It was **just a thought**," Tobin says, frowning.

"Tell me. A **shot in the dark** is **better than nothing**."

Tobin's face brightens. "Well," he says. "It will require you to help me with something."

You are suspicious. "Look, if you're trying to **squeeze me**—"

"It involves **getting back at** Frankie for what he's **put me through**," Tobin says.

"Hey, **that's your business**. I don't want to get involved—"

"It **cuts both ways**. If Frankie isn't my problem anymore, then he won't be *your* problem either. Anyways, I've got **something up my sleeve**."

Go to **page 96**.

The ex-cop is admitting he is corrupt, and you shouldn't trust him. Besides, the way these two are talking gives you a **bad feeling** about them. Not only does it seem strange that one of the guards has no French accent, but how can you trust a former police officer who lost his job because he was dishonest? You decide not to trust the **dirty cop** or his companion, especially after what you heard from the other guards in the alley.

You decide to stay quiet for now and wait for their **smoke break** to end. After they walk back into the museum, you get out of the dumpster and **brush off** your clothes. You look at where the two men stood. Several cigarette butts lie on the ground.

You think about returning to the museum and **heading back** to the service door.

For a door that shouldn't be opened, there sure are a lot of people using it today.

You pull on the handle, but the door doesn't budge. The rogue guards must have secured it when they went back in. You can think of only one other option: the door left wide open at the other end of the alley—the one that Maddy and her crew **broke into**.

Metal pieces from the lock have been **torched off** and left on the ground. You step over the debris and find yourself inside a room dimly lit by red lights. You watch and listen for **any signs** of Maddy and her crew, but all you notice are stacks of unused office furniture along the wall and some office equipment. Electrical gauges line the brick walls, while various pipes **run along** the ceiling toward a long corridor. You peek into the corridor and see an entrance to the parking garage. A single room in the distance looks like an office for the parking garage staff. You return to examining the area around you, finding a desk by the door holding a few stacks of papers, a lamp, and a phone. You immediately sprint to it and **pick up** the receiver to dial the operator. No dial tone. You look down and see that the phone's cord has been **cut in two**. You check the lamp and computer. Neither one **turns on**. The **power is out**.

*Those guys must have **cut the power and phone lines***.

A generator must be powering the red lights around the room, and you wonder whether the main museum building is running on generators as well. You continue to scan for resources or anything that might be helpful.

A curious set of grooves on the floor in the corner **catches your eye**. As you get closer, you see it is a metal hatch in the floor. You grip the handle on the hatch and pull. The metal door groans as you **swing it open**. There is a ladder along a wall that descends into the darkness, but you can barely see beyond six steps down. This must be a service tunnel that goes beneath the museum.

Down the corridor from the parking garage, you hear footsteps approaching. You quickly dash under the desk in between a wastebasket and a box of tools.

"I think I left my blowtorch in the office," someone says.

"You're such an idiot, Tobin."

"I'm sorry, Frankie. There's just too much **going on** today."

Frankie.

Your blood begins to boil, but what can you do? They outnumber you, **two to one**.

"It's not just today. You've been making a lot of mistakes, and it's starting to **piss off** Maddy. She only **keeps you around** because you're the crew's engineer. Got that? If you keep **screwing up**, she may have to rethink whether the **benefits outweigh the costs**."

You look out from behind the desk and **spot** a blowtorch in the far corner of the room.

"There it is," Tobin says with a sigh of relief. He enters the maintenance office.

"See? That's evidence that could have been used against us," Frankie growls. "That's **asking for trouble**."

"I know, I know. It won't happen again."

You listen as Tobin apologizes again and walks over to the blowtorch.

"Is there anything else around here that belongs to you?"

"No," Tobin says, shuffling his feet. "That's all."

"What about that service hatch? The one Francois went into. Why the hell is it **wide open**?" Frankie's foot taps the floor—*tap, tap, tap.*

"I'll **take care of it**," Tobin says hurriedly.

Your **heart races** as he approaches your **hiding spot**. You can see his legs from under the desk.

Frankie pounds something with his fists. "Come here, Tobin!" he yells.

You hear the sickening sound of someone getting slapped in the face. *Thwack!*

"This is so ridiculous," Frankie continues. "Tell me you were wearing gloves when you opened the hatch earlier? Tell me you didn't leave any fingerprints in here? You are so **off your game** today you might as well sign your name on a photo to leave for the cops!"

Tobin's voice trembles. "Yeah, yeah. I was wearing gloves!"

"Sure?"

Tobin hesitates. "Maybe. Yeah! Now that I think about it, I think I did," Tobin mumbles.

"You think? Go **wipe down** that hatch and make sure it's closed," Frankie roars. "And check around again."

Exposed under the desk, you start to feel unsafe. Tobin is now busy checking the room and **wiping things down**. Any moment he might crouch to the floor and see you hiding under the desk. You consider **making a dash** for the hatch and diving into the service tunnel, but you know they will see you. There are a few heavy wrenches in the toolbox near you, but you doubt you could **take out** Frankie and Tobin together.

"Stop yelling at me, Frankie," Tobin says, his voice quivering. This time you hear rage, not fear.

"Or what?" Frankie mocks. "Are you going to snitch to Maddy about it?"

"Or else I'm going to take this blowtorch and **seal your mouth shut**!"

Frankie laughs hysterically.

"I swear I'll do it!"

"Blowtorch my mouth shut," Frankie says, mocking Tobin. He spits on the floor in disgust. "Go ahead and **give it a try**. I'd like to see that."

Frankie's challenge only makes Tobin angrier. You suddenly hear the blowtorch being **fired up**. Frankie stops laughing. Tobin waves the blowtorch at Frankie, **lighting up** the room's walls with blue and orange light. Even from under the desk, you can feel the heat from the flame.

"All right, all right," Frankie says, suddenly concerned. "Don't **botch it up** for yourself, Tobin. I'm warning you . . ."

You consider again using the heavy wrenches in the toolbox. If Frankie and Tobin were to fight, you could **jump into action** and **catch them by surprise**. You might even be able to get Tobin **on your side** at this point, judging by how much he hates Frankie. But the blowtorch makes you hesitate. The hot flame flutters as Tobin waves it from side to side. Frankie grunts and bumps into the desk, knocking the phone onto the floor in front of you.

They're actually fighting each other. Maybe I should just stay out of the way . . .

If you **wait it out** long enough, **the problem might take care of itself**.

Something metallic rattles and falls onto the floor. The roar of the blowtorch **goes out**. Three quick thuds follow—the sounds of someone getting punched rapidly. Something hits the desk hard, and for a terrifying moment, you think the desk will be **split open** on top of you.

Tobin gasps in pain as Frankie hits him. "You **got it out of your system** now?" he says. "Well, did you?"

Thwack. Another slap in the face.

Tobin mumbles an answer, and Frankie orders him to **clean up**. Boxes and cans are kicked around.

"And make sure you **leave no trace**, or I will make sure Maddy agrees to get rid of you!"

Frankie walks back into the corridor, leaving Tobin sniffling to himself. More boxes and cans are kicked about the room.

"Someday," Tobin says quietly to no one. "I'll **show you who's boss**."

If you think that Tobin is planning on alerting the boss, Maddy, about Frankie, go to **page 78**.

If you think that Tobin is venting about how he wants to retaliate against Frankie, go to **page 93**.

Maddy has ordered her men to protect whomever they find. Maddy's voice is soft and quiet as she commands the guards. You remember the conversation you had with her in the line for the main exhibit. She seemed so calm and professional.

You decide to wait and see what will happen. Anyway, right now you are too afraid to move. You hope the guards will help you if they see you. **Just to be on the safe side**, you conceal yourself with some discarded cardboard boxes leaning against the dumpster.

The footsteps come closer. You put your hand over your mouth to quiet your breathing and wish suddenly that you could just disappear. You **close your eyes tight** when you hear a man rapping his knuckles against the side of the dumpster. The thudding noise explodes near your ears.

Suddenly, you hear the sound of squeaking and panic.

"What the—rats!" a guard wails as his boots start stomping on the ground. You hear something darting out from under the dumpster, **heading in all directions**.

"Gah! I hate rats!"

You **peek out** from under the lid and see that the rodents have disappeared down a storm drain.

The scared guards run back to the group.

"Losers!" someone teases, laughing.

The crew **turns its attention** back to the door at the end of the alley, and you go back to watching them, making sure to stay even quieter than before. Maddy puts on her black coat, while the rest of the guards stuff items into their duffel bags.

The sound of flames searing through metal continues for a few more seconds until you hear a metal bar drop to the ground. The man with the blowtorch steps away, and another person with a crowbar **takes his place**. The man shoves the metal rod into the door's frame. More metallic parts clatter to the ground as the door is finally pried open.

"Inside," Maddy commands.

The men walk through, **one by one**.

You wait **with bated breath** and consider your next move. You can check the other door leading back into the museum, or you can follow Maddy's group through the busted door and hope it leads you somewhere outside the museum and to freedom.

Which way do I go?

You look at the dumpster, and your **skin crawls** when you remember the rats that came **pouring out** from under it. You will be glad to leave your hiding place soon enough.

You check the door leading back to the museum and find that it has been locked.

*Oh, well. So much for that. I guess it's further **down the rabbit hole** for me...*

You have only one other option left, so you tiptoe over to the door that Maddy went through. Hearing nothing coming from the inside, you **poke your head through** the entrance and walk in.

Go to **page 98**.

The guard is asking you to stop arguing with him and to surrender quietly. You worry about the noise you both are making, and you decide it is better to let the guard **have his way**.

You lift your hands over your head. "All right, all right," you tell the guard.

"That is right, criminal! Do not move or else," the guard warns, shining the flashlight in your face.

"Look," you tell him as calmly as possible. "I repeat: I'm not a criminal. I'm just a tourist looking for a friend."

"Right. And I am the girl with a pearl earring," he says sarcastically.

"My friend was taken, and I need your help."

The guard's hands are shaking, and he drops his flashlight. It hits the floor with a loud pop before rolling away. It is too late; someone has heard. Loud footsteps come running toward the gift shop.

Before you can do anything, the guard shrieks and **jumps to his feet** from behind the counter. "Please! Do not hurt me!" he cries out.

"We found another one," a woman says.

"These guys are like roaches—they keep **popping up out of nowhere**," her male companion **chimes in**.

You can hear the poor guard's knees begin to **knock together** as he struggles to **keep his balance**.

"**Who else is around?**" the woman asks. "Speak!"

You **hold your breath**. Next to you, the guard is **tongue-tied**.

"Tell us the truth, or we'll **take matters into our own hands**."

> If you think that the intruders are only saying they will take the guard into custody if he isn't honest with them, go to **page 90**.

> If you think that the intruders are threatening to harm the guard if he isn't honest with them, go to **page 103**.

The intruders are only saying they will take the guard into custody if he isn't honest with them. Maybe they don't mean him any real harm. For now, you decide not to reveal yourself by staying crouched down and **out of sight**.

From the dark recess behind the counter, you watch as a masked man approaches the terrified guard and calmly kicks his flashlight **out of reach**. His partner, a woman also wearing a mask, **picks it up** and orders the guard to move away.

When they move toward him, you realize that they have sinister intentions. They aren't only going to take him into custody; they will probably hurt him if he doesn't **speak up**.

Your **heart races**, but you are still **frozen with fear**. The guard begins to tremble, scared for his life. Then he bolts, desperately trying to escape. The masked man catches him, and they both tussle on the ground. Eventually, the guard manages to **slip away**, and the masked assailant chases after him.

You **peek out** from behind the counter but see no one. You count to five, listening for any movement. Thinking **it is clear**, you **get to your feet**. When you **turn around**, you find yourself **face to face** with the masked woman. It seems she has been waiting for you to **pop your head up** all along. She smiles knowingly at you. Not sure what else to do, you raise your arms in the air.

She talks into her walkie-talkie, her eyes **looking you up and down**. "I knew he wasn't alone," she says into the device. The gun in her other hand is **trained on you**. "There's a scared guard **running around**, and I've got a tourist with me. I'm in the gift shop. Second floor."

To your relief, she lowers the gun and **puts it away**. Slowly, you lower your hands. The woman smiles and points the flashlight at you. "We meet again," she says.

"Who—who are you?"

"Don't you recognize me?" she asks.

You squint in the low light. With a dramatic **sweep of her arm**, the woman **takes off** her mask. You recognize the short black hair and dazzling green eyes.

"Maddy?" you say, astounded.

Maddy **throws back** her head and laughs, just like she did when you first met her in line for the main exhibit. "Oh, good!" she says. "**Points** for remembering my name."

"What are you doing here?" you ask her. "What's all this about?"

"**Just the usual**," she says, shrugging her shoulders and tilting her head to the side nonchalantly. "Admiring the artwork. Stealing a painting." She walks to a shelf filled with souvenirs, moving with an **air of confidence**. "So?"

"So, what?" you ask.

"What's it like **being in the presence** of the world's greatest art thief?"

"I've, uh, never heard of you," you tell her honestly. Then you cringe, realizing you might have offended her.

Maddy laughs, though you can tell her **ego is bruised**. "I'm the reason museums have security measures."

Your **mind goes blank**, and all you can manage to do is to state the obvious. "You're trying to steal the *Girl with a Pearl Earring*."

"Trying?" Now she sounds insulted. She looks you in the eye. "This one's going to be a **piece of cake**. And I've never been close to getting caught." Maddy **clicks off** her flashlight, and your eyes readjust. "*Trying*! Hah!"

Even in the dark, you can see the outline of her shoulders and the curve of her hip. Before, at the main exhibit, Maddy looked like a burnt marshmallow in her oversized black coat.

"What happened to your coat?" you ask.

Maddy puts her hands on her hips and pretends to model for you. "I took it off," she says. "Too much stuff in the pockets, you know what I mean?" Her laugh is as sharp as the look in her eyes. "Now, come with me. I have a painting to steal." She walks behind you and prods you forward with her flashlight.

"Just let me go, Maddy," you plead. "All I wanted to do today was find my friends and get out of here. I don't care about you or the painting."

She purses her lips. "I'm definitely not letting you go," she says. "I'll **let you in on a secret**. There's a reason I've never been caught. It's simple: I never **leave anything to chance**. In case **there's a snag**, you'll be my **bargaining chip**."

She's taking me hostage.

Ahead of you, Maddy's masked partner returns and looks surprised to see you. "I **chased down** that guard and tied him up pretty good," he says, huffing and puffing. "And I also found Willie."

"Willie? Where?" Maddy says.

"**Tied up** somewhere." The man gives you an accusing look.

Further off, you hear someone else approaching with heavy steps. *Willie.* Your **blood runs cold**.

His face as red as a tomato, Willie points at you threateningly. "There you are!" he says, running toward you at full-speed.

Every thought in your head screams at you to **run like mad**.

"A reunion!" Maddy says, delighted.

Willie **stops short** when he sees Maddy standing next to you. He is seething with rage. The very presence of Maddy seems to **keep him in check** though. He is unsure what to do while Maddy is there, watching.

You start to **move away**, but Maddy puts a hand on your shoulder. She whispers in your ear, "Don't move. I've **got a handle on it**."

If you think that Maddy has another weapon in her hand, go to **page 109**.

If you think that Maddy is in control of the situation, go to **page 112**.

Tobin is venting about how he wants to retaliate against Frankie. You decide you want to help Tobin. You know exactly how he feels because you have had your **share of** bullies too, and you try to avoid conflict whenever you can. How many times have you wished you were more powerful, more confident, and more in control? If you were Frankie's boss, you would force him to apologize to Tobin.

Tobin must be feeling weak and small after the **dress down** he got from Frankie. You realize this might be your opportunity **to take advantage of the situation**. Perhaps you can **plant a seed** of revenge in Tobin's mind and get his cooperation.

"You're right," you say, **coming out** from under the desk. "Frankie shouldn't **pick on you** like that."

"Who said that?" Tobin says, **spinning around**. He grabs the blowtorch and waves it at you.

The torch is unlit. You **put up your hands** to show him you **mean him no harm**, but his eyes dart **to and fro** wildly. As you approach Tobin, your toe kicks at something. You **bend down** and **pick up** a pair of glasses.

"These yours?" you ask, holding them out. Tobin's hand reaches out, and you place the glasses within reach.

"Thanks," he says. One of the lenses is broken, but he seems to be relieved to be wearing his glasses again.

"Thank you," you tell him. "I'm the one you saved in the alleyway earlier. You convinced Frankie to **put me in** the dumpster instead of getting rid of me. I **owe you my life**."

You reach out your hand, but Tobin **jumps** back. "Stop right there," he says.

"I'm not trying to **start any trouble**. I have nothing against you and your friend."

"Friend?" Tobin says with disgust all over his face. "I hate that guy!"

"Frankie?" you ask. "Aren't you two partners?"

"It's not a partnership."

"Yeah, he was terrible to you," you say.

Tobin's arms drop, and he shrugs at you. In the low light, you can see blood trickling from his nose.

"He always **throws his weight around** and acts like the king of thieves," he continues. Tobin wipes his nose on his sleeve. "Who are you anyway? And why were you in that alleyway?"

"I, uh—"

"I bet I know. You probably followed Frankie after he pickpocketed you. I knew he'd get caught eventually. It's a ritual of his."

"I just want to get out of here," you interrupt, forgetting about your wallet and phone. "You have to help."

Tobin looks apologetic. "Sorry, that's impossible. All the entrances and exits will be sealed by now. We run a **tight ship**. Nobody gets in or out."

"Not even you?" you ask.

"Well, I mean, of course *I* can get out of here," Tobin stammers. "But you? **Fat chance**. Not while we're stealing the *Girl with a Pearl Earring*." Tobin pauses. "Oops. I probably shouldn't have told you that."

"I don't care about what you're doing here," you try to reassure him. "I just want out." You dare not mention your friends.

Better for him to think I'm alone.

"You can leave when we're all done. You should probably go back to hiding in that dumpster. It's probably the safest place in the entire museum right now."

Tobin wipes his nose on his sleeve again, and he begins to wipe the blood spots on the floor with a handkerchief. Seeing all the blood suddenly makes you nervous for your safety.

"Anyway, we're not killers," Tobin says with a snort. "A couple of guys in the crew are violent jerks like Frankie, but Maddy **would go nuts** if we added murder to our list of crimes. Interpol would **double down on us** if we ever left a dead body."

"Well, I guess I'm glad for that," you say, partly relieved.

"Most of the tourists and visitors have been evacuated. We might take a few as hostage if there's a big problem, but we've never had a big problem." Tobin stares at you for a moment. "Well, until now."

You let out a deep sigh. "I'm not going back in the dumpster."

"I know," Tobin says. "I doubt I could force you to go back anyway. It would take a Frankie or a Barrett. And I don't **have the stomach**."

"With or without your help, I'm going to get out of here."

"Good luck then," he tells you, as he sits against the wall. "If I could ask a favor, just don't go to the police right away. Wait a few hours, so we have a **head start**."

"I'd be more inclined to **keep my mouth shut** if you helped me," you say, hoping for some bargaining leverage.

"I'd be more inclined to help if I believed that," Tobin replies. His eyes stare sadly at the bloodstains smeared on the floor.

You get a **sudden burst** of inspiration and **snap your fingers**. "How about this: I'll help you **clean up** here. That makes me an accomplice, right? If you get caught, then you can **snitch on me**." You hope Tobin **buys it**. To your relief, his face **brightens**.

"You know, that's not such a bad idea," Tobin says, scratching his chin. "I could use your help. It might get me into Maddy's **good graces** and take Frankie **out of the picture**."

"Tell me what you **have in mind**," you say.

Tobin's eyes **flash** with determination. "I've **got a few tricks up my sleeve**," he says.

If you think that Tobin is talking about having weapons to help fight Frankie, go to **page 96**.

If you think that Tobin has a few ideas to take revenge on Frankie, go to **page 100**.

You guess that Tobin is talking about having weapons to help **fight** Frankie. "I suppose **we can take** Frankie if we fight him together," you say excitedly. "Now, what do you **have up your sleeve** that can **help us out**?"

"What?" Tobin asks, confused.

"You're talking about fighting him, right? With weapons?" you say, **puffing out your chest** a bit.

"We are not fighting Frankie. I meant I had some *ideas*. A plan. As you can see, I'm not a strong person. That means I have to be smarter."

"Oh," you say as Tobin looks at you angrily. You **laugh it off**, "That's totally what I meant."

"**Don't get me wrong**," Tobin says. "Frankie deserves a good old-fashioned **beatdown**."

"So, what's your plan?" you ask.

Tobin rubs his chin and then points at you with both fingers. "Frankie and I are **in charge** of stealing cars in the parking garage. Now, what you might not know is that new cars are all computerized. You press the gas; a computer tells the car to **speed up**."

You scratch your head and shrug. "I thought everything was mechanical."

"I'm going to assume that this is all new to you," Tobin says. "I could hack into a car with my laptop and control everything, from the alarms and steering, to the braking and signaling. The newer the car, the less mechanical it is in a way. You'd be surprised to **find out** how much we rely on computers when we drive."

"You can control cars, but what does that get us?"

"After we sneak you into the parking garage, I'll distract Frankie with something—maybe another mistake for him to yell at me for. You get into one of the cars, and when Frankie and I **jump** the other cars, I'll program your car and **chart a course** to take you away from the museum."

"Where will it take me, exactly?" you ask.

"Somewhere far away from here," Tobin answers.

He starts pulling out the toolbox from under the desk and selects several wrenches, wipes them clean, and then gives you several to hold. "Now, if you don't mind . . ." he starts to say.

"Sure," you say. You grip the wrenches. "This is actually a brilliant plan," you add, hoping to keep him encouraged and motivated.

"Oh, totally," Tobin says, staring eagerly at the tools in your hands.

"What do you want to do with these?" you ask, waving the wrenches. "I thought your plan involves computers."

Tobin smiles and holds out his hand. You place the tools back onto a handkerchief in his palm. Tobin **clears his throat** and places the tools back into the box.

"The **deal is sealed**. Thank you," he says.

"What?" you ask, feeling a sudden rush of dread.

"You'll forgive me if I don't totally trust you."

You realize now why Tobin gave you the tools to hold. Fingerprints—your fingerprints are all over the thieves' tools now.

"See, I'm hoping you don't go to the police when I decide to let you go. In fact, I'm hoping you leave France and never come back. We're all **in the same boat** now."

If you think that Tobin is talking about escaping overseas—and possibly taking you with him, go to **page 125**.

If you think that Tobin is saying you are now in the same situation as he is, go to **page 132**.

You take measured and quiet steps through the door. A crumpled piece of paper caught in a draft flutters toward you. You quickly **pick it up** and examine it. Red ink is scribbled all over the paper. You realize that you are seeing a crude sketch of the museum's layout. Hand-drawn arrows point to various rooms. A large red circle encircles the largest room at the center.

The main exhibit.

You put the map in your pocket and **look around**. You are in an office of some kind. An empty desk is **tucked away** in a corner at one end. The walls are built with old brick. The air smells musty and stale. Gauges and switches **line the walls** that lead to a large control box with blinking red lights. This must be the electrical room, you decide. Another corridor off to the side leads to the parking garage. Maddy and her men must be **plotting an escape route** out of the museum from here.

You **double back** to the entrance near the busted door to investigate further and find a phone that has been knocked off the desk. You check for a dial tone, but the **line is dead**.

Then you notice something odd. On the floor, drawn in faint chalk, is an arrow. You trace the arrow and see that it points to a metal trapdoor built right into the floor. You kick the heavy metal cover, and it jiggles in place. It must be a hatch to a service tunnel that goes underground beneath the museum.

You are busy testing the hatch cover when a tense conversation from the passageway leading to the parking garage erupts and **breaks the silence**.

"How long do we have to wait?" someone complains.

"You know what? You've been making a lot of stupid mistakes, and I'm **getting sick of it**."

"I'm getting nervous with all this waiting. We go to a room. Wait. Walk through the emergency exit. Wait. Go to the garage. Stand here and—guess what—wait!"

"Are you done whining?"

Down the Rabbit Hole

You need an **exit strategy**. You study the metal hatch in the floor. You tug at the latch, but it refuses to budge. It looks like it is stuck.

"You wanted to join the floor crew. No one said you had to put in some manual labor. That was all you. Now, **shut up**, and do what we tell you."

You **take another look** at the hatch cover. A locking mechanism keeps it **stuck in place**. With a flick, the dead bolt **slides out** easily. You **swing open** the hatch cover and look down. The entrance to the service tunnel reveals a deep hole that drops to an underground level.

"Go back to the office and collect our tools."

The men are very close to entering the room.

Here goes nothing . . .

You **take one last look** down into the dark hole in the floor and then hoist yourself onto the ladder.

Go to **page 122**.

"Okay, let's hear it," you tell Tobin. "What's the plan?"

Tobin stares at you blankly for a moment.

"Tobin?" you say, snapping your fingers in front of his face. "You said you have a plan."

"Oh, yes," he says, shaking his head. "Let me **start from the top. Do you mind**?"

You give Tobin an impatient look but decide to **humor him**. "Try to be quick. Frankie might come back and give us both a beating."

"Right," Tobin agrees. "Earlier, we had the fire alarms go off so we could evacuate the museum and garage. Problem is, you can only keep people away from their cars for so long. That's what our security guard friends have been doing."

You **clear your throat** to interrupt. "One question," you ask. "You said something about security guard friends?"

"We **paid off** some of the museum security guards. They're working for us now," Tobin says. "As long as the security guards **do their jobs** keeping people out and away from the museum, the rest of the crew can **go to work** on the painting."

"And what about us?" you say, steering Tobin back to the plan to get you out of the museum.

"I start **hacking** the vehicles using my laptop and some controllers. New cars these days are more computerized than ever—"

"**Get on with it**," you interrupt again. "We don't **have all day**."

"If I can control the cars with my computer, that means we don't need a fleet of drivers. Just me and Frankie," Tobin says, his voice **speeding up**.

"And me?"

"And you . . ." Tobin says, his voice **trailing off**. "Yes! You'll go into one car with a controller. It's basically a tablet computer with a GPS system and some extra buttons. I designed the software myself. It's actually very easy to use. Even a big gorilla like Frankie can learn how to use it quickly."

"Give me a **quick rundown**," you tell Tobin.

"Well, one of the things I'm thinking you can do is hide in a vehicle with Frankie—"

"No way," you say, **cutting him off**.

"—and wait until he's vulnerable. Then you could **bash him in the head** or something like that."

"Didn't you hear me? Not a good plan. No head bashing."

"Right, right," Tobin says. "Okay, a better plan would be to control his seat, move him closer to the wheel, and then **set off** the airbag. That would **knock him out** pretty good, don't you think?"

You nod your head in agreement. "That's a better plan."

"I'll program the car to drive to an undisclosed station where you can **slip out**," Tobin says, beaming **ear to ear**. "I'll send the police there while we thieves escape with our goods."

"**What's the catch?**"

"The controller I give you will only let you do a few things. I can't have you changing the plan."

"I understand," you tell him. "What do we need to do first?"

"We clean this room, hack a few more cars, and then load them up with everything the crew has brought out to be packed into the vehicles. The faster we do this, the more Maddy will be pleased with me."

For the first time since you have met him, Tobin looks confident and sure of himself.

"How do you know so much about this stuff?" you ask.

"I was brought into the crew for my tech and computer knowledge," Tobin answers. "Maddy has her oversized henchmen for the physical stuff. I'm her technical expert."

"How did you get into stealing paintings? A guy with your kind of talents could be making millions creating apps."

"I used to work in an accounting department. One day, I used my talents to route some of the company money into my bank account. I'm not exactly a **white hat**," Tobin says, embarrassed.

After you **clean up** and gather the needed computer equipment, you and Tobin sneak into the parking garage and walk down a level. Tobin tells you to wait while he surveys the area.

"The **coast is clear**," he says. "Frankie's **loading up** the cars on another level, so we can start hacking in. Let's go."

You follow Tobin carefully. You watch for guards and anyone else, but Tobin reassures you. "The guards will think you're **with me**. It's Frankie we have to **watch out for**. I think **covered all the bases**, but I did forget one thing: I never got your name."

"It's Sammy," you tell him.

"Nice to meet you, Sammy. Now, let's go steal a few cars."

As you walk past a group of guards, you nod and try to look as natural as possible. "It's all about **how you carry yourself**," you remember Darla saying to you once in another one of her pep talks.

Your stand a little taller, but then you feel your **heart sink**. Darla and Eric are still out there. If you stay with Tobin, you know there is a good chance of you leaving the museum undetected. Outside, you can go get help and alert the police of the hostages, so they don't **storm the place** and make the thieves panic.

"Sammy?" Tobin says. "You **zoned out**. What's wrong?"

"Are you sure this is the best plan for us?" you ask.

"Yeah, the best, considering our goals."

But my goal is finding my friends and making sure they're safe . . .

"Right," you say quietly.

"**Look sharp**. We have to **deliver the goods** on this one."

If you think that Tobin means you should do what is expected of you and follow the original plan, go to **page 133**.

If you think that Tobin is only thinking about the loot they will be stealing, and it is better not to trust him, go to **page 191**.

The intruders are threatening to harm the guard if he isn't honest with them. You can't let them **take matters into their own hands**. You are scared for the terrified guard. You decide to reveal yourself and hope for the best. You **crawl out** from behind the counter with your **hands in the air**. One of the masked strangers continues to bully the security guard, while the other **turns her attention** to you.

"Hey! Leave him alone," you tell them.

The masked male **looks up**, surprised at your presence. "The **toy cop**'s friend reveals himself," he says.

"Just let him go," you say, your voice quavering. You try your hardest to sound tough by lowering your voice, but the two intruders stare at you without flinching.

"Move," the female intruder orders you, calmly taking a gun out of her pocket and pointing it at you. "Move to the corner!"

You do as she says. Meanwhile, the frightened guard **sees an opening** and charges at the masked male, slamming him with his shoulder. The intruder flies across the room. Freed from his captor, the guard **takes off running** out of the gift shop. The masked man **gets on his feet** and goes after him in **hot pursuit**.

The female intruder shouts after her partner, and you take advantage of the distraction by taking the gun from her hands.

"Hey!" she whines, upset that you **got the upper hand**.

"A fake," you tell her, pulling the gun apart and dropping the plastic pieces to the floor.

She puts her hands on her hips and regards you with cold disdain. With a graceful calm, she takes her walkie-talkie, twists the dial, and speaks into it. "I need someone in the East Wing to come help me. Second floor. Gift shop."

You look to the door, and the woman steps in front of the entrance.

"I wouldn't if I were you," she says. With a sweep of her arm, she **takes off** her mask with a flourish and reveals herself.

"Maddy?" you say, shocked.

"Indeed. The world-famous art thief **in the flesh**," she says triumphantly.

You can't **believe your eyes**. Your words come out in spurts. "Back at the main exhibit. We were standing in line. We talked. Wow."

Maddy squints in the dark. "Glad you remembered. And here I thought you were just a normal, boring tourist. Took me a while, but I was thinking this whole time that you looked a little familiar." She chuckles. "Strange. I'm almost glad to see you."

"Why were you wearing a mask?" you ask her.

"Is it overkill? I'm kind of dramatic like that," she says, pointing at herself. "And I'm **kind of a big deal**."

Like before, Maddy looks as striking as ever. But you notice a more eccentric streak in her behavior now.

"We try to wear the masks while we **clear out**. Keeps people from recognizing us."

"But you just revealed yourself to me," you say.

Maddy shrugs and laughs again. She gives you an expression as if to say, "Oops."

You step back away nervously. If you've seen her face, what will she do to you?

"Once in a while, you just have to be honest and say, 'Hey, you might not know this about me, but I steal paintings **for a living**.'" She laughs again, sounding a little **unhinged**.

You **brace yourself against** the gift shop's wall while Maddy looks at a table filled with souvenir mugs.

"**What I wouldn't give** for some more coffee," Maddy says, looking longingly at the mugs.

"What I wouldn't give to start this day over," you respond.

Maddy turns to you again, her expression serious now. "You're not Interpol, are you?"

You ignore her question.

"My instincts say no, but I heard someone might be here looking for me today." Maddy takes a mug off the shelf and feels for her pockets.

"Looks like you could use your big coat," you say.

"What?"

"Where's your big coat?"

"Oh, that. Somewhere," she says. She pulls out her walkie-talkie. "This is Maddy. Where is that escort for my hostage?" she demands. Then she turns to you. "I would escort you myself, but I have other things to attend to."

"I'm on my way," a voice responds over the walkie-talkie. The speaker **cuts out** with some static.

Maddy watches you as you look over her shoulder out into the museum. You can't let yourself be taken. You have to escape now.

Seemingly **reading your thoughts**, Maddy warns you, "Don't even."

You **look her over** to **size her up**. You shift your weight to the **balls of your feet**. *What if I just try to tackle her? She's tiny. I could take her.*

Behind her, you see two people now running toward the gift shop. One of them is the masked man that accompanied Maddy before. The other person is Willie.

You feel your **blood run cold**.

Maddy reaches into her pocket for something. Is it a weapon?

"Looking to **make a fast break**?" she asks, sensing your fear.

If you think that Maddy knows you are looking for a way to escape, go to **page 109**.

If you think that Maddy believes you are going to try to break something to cause a distraction, go to **page 205**.

Eric means that working together will be enough to **take on** the art thieves.

"Fine," you say.

Eric **holds up** his hand. You reluctantly give him a **high-five**. He quietly goes back to the storage closet and returns, dragging a duffel bag behind him.

"**Check this out**," Eric says, pulling out a security guard shirt. "I was going to grab some makeshift weapons, but I found this stuffed under the shelves."

Eric **takes off** his sweater and **puts on** one of the dark green uniforms. He digs through the bag, grabs another shirt, and tosses it to you. "This should fit," he says.

"You're insane," you tell Eric. The uniform feels cheap, like a costume replica.

"I know," Eric says. He rummages through the bag some more and finds a pair of crudely tailored slacks. "This is going to be awesome."

From afar, fully clothed, he looks like an ordinary security guard. **Up close**, he looks like a cheap imitation.

"I remember seeing some of the guards earlier," you say. "Something about them **stood out**. Now I know why. We look like we're wearing Halloween costumes."

"**Good eye**. See, this is what happens when no one **pays attention**," Eric says. "They **let the bad in with the good**."

Eric finds a flashlight in the bag and **shows off** by flipping it in the air. "This way," he says, walking to the door at the end of the hallway.

Testing the knob, you find that it is locked.

"I **have just the thing**," Eric says, jingling his set of keys.

The next room is a large storeroom of appliances and museum gear. Glass displays are pushed up against the wall, and stacks of empty frames litter the room, along with piles of shelving. Eric steps over a pile of plastic wrap, shining his flashlight on the dusty display cases. The air is cold and musty, and you **get the feeling** that no one has been inside here in a long time.

"Nothing happening here," Eric says.

"You sound disappointed."

"Only a little," he says, chuckling.

His laughter is cut short when a door opens on the far side of the storeroom. You and Eric **take cover**, sliding behind a set of shelves. Two men hurry through the room, too preoccupied to notice you.

"*Où avez-vous vu pour la dernière vos clés?*"

"*Je ne me souviens pas.*"

One of the guards stops when his walkie-talkie buzzes. He puts the receiver to his ear and spins in your direction. Eric pulls you back just **in time**, and you pull your knees to your chest, making yourself as small as possible.

"Team seven, location?" a voice demands over the walkie-talkie.

The guards start to argue for a moment before one of them responds in accented English. "We—we are near the, uh, offices."

"Still?" the gruff voice asks over the walkie-talkie.

"Actually, we are finished here, I think," the guard says, unsure.

"Good. Go meet the others and do another **sweep** of the Main Hall. Make sure all the visitors are gone. Do this right and Maddy will reward you handsomely."

"Oh, of course! Please tell her we are, uh, grateful for this, uh, opportunity," the shaky guard says. He is clearly intimidated by the voice on the other end.

"Stupid!" one of the guards says to himself. He **runs his mouth off** with a few more French curse words you can only guess the meaning of. The other guard begins to speak, but the louder guard **cuts him off**. They soon leave the room the way they entered.

"Seems like they were **rattled**," you say, "as if someone lost their keys and had to find them, perhaps?"

"Hey, we're only out of that closet because of them," Eric says, holding the key ring and jiggling it.

"The voice on the walkie-talkie said something about Maddy..." you start to say.

"So?"

"I met someone named Maddy when I was in line for the main exhibit," you explain.

"You met the queen of the thieves!" Eric says excitedly.

In any other situation, you would laugh, but the seriousness of it all keeps you from even **breaking a smile**.

"Well, what did she look like?"

"I was in line for the main exhibit, and she was standing behind me," you say, trying to remember. "We talked for a few minutes. She had these amazing green eyes."

"What else?"

"Dark hair. Red lips," you describe. "She wore a big heavy coat. She also had this laugh." You imitate Maddy by throwing your head back and cackling.

"Um, that's very descriptive," Eric says dryly. "Looks like you had an interesting encounter with this woman. Anything else?"

You sigh wistfully. "I can't stop seeing those green eyes."

"Well, she sounds like those art nerds you used to **hang out** with in high school," Eric jokes. "So serious. All the time. Serious."

"**Play nice**," you warn him.

"Well, if you see her, **point her out**. We'll **take our chances**. Right now, we have a **window of opportunity**."

If you think that Eric believes you have an advantage over the thieves and should do something now, go to **page 111**.

If you think that Eric is talking about escaping out of a window in the museum at the next opportunity, go to **page 155**.

You run, looking to **make a fast break**, and you do exactly what Maddy doesn't expect you to do: You run **straight at her**, charging forward like a runaway train.

"Oof!" she grunts as you **knock her over**.

It looks like she doesn't have a weapon on her, but you decide not to **stick around** and check. You make a **mad dash for it**. Behind you, you hear Maddy yell in fury, "**Sic 'em**, Willie! Don't let him escape!"

You come to a hallway lined with galleries. Unfortunately, most of them are **locked down**. You test several of the metal security gates at a few entrances, but they are all too heavy to lift. It seems that most of the museum has been **sectioned off** into a jumble of hallways and corridors, reminding you of a mall after all the stores have closed.

Your legs ache, and your sides are starting to cramp, but you have to keep on running. Willie is **hot on your trail**. If you rest for just a moment, you aren't sure you will be able to get back up.

You continue on. Up ahead, there is an intersection. To the left are more galleries; off to the side, bathrooms. You veer left and flip a bench, creating an obstacle behind you. Further on, a set of galleries with their security gates only half-lowered look like they might provide something of a **hiding spot**.

Eventually, you find yourself in a gallery filled with woven fabrics hanging from the ceiling and draping down the walls. You read the sign.

Tapisseries

The Tapestries gallery. *Perfect.*

You dive under the gate and find a place to hide among the displays. Willie is nowhere **in sight**, but you can hear him grumbling in the distance.

"I'm tired of playing this **cat and mouse game**," he keeps saying.

It is only a **matter of time** before he reaches the gallery and checks behind every single drape of fabric. The bathrooms are another option, but you will be **cornered** if he finds you there.

Looking around, you see another gallery filled with display cases of ancient clay vases. One display is already broken with some artifacts missing from its shelf. Reaching in, you **pick up** several of the bigger vessels, testing their weight and strength.

You can hear Willie coming closer. It is time to **come to grips** with your situation.

If you decide to grab a vase to use as a weapon against Willie, go to **page 120**.

If you realize that you need to be more cautious and consider your options more carefully, go to **page 131**.

Eric believes you have an advantage over the thieves and should do something now. They have no idea that you will be coming for them. It is a big **edge** you can't waste.

"You're right," you tell him. "If we find a way to stop her, the rest of her team will **fall apart**."

"I'm glad you **see things my way**," Eric says. "If this Maddy woman is truly the **brains of this operation**, then taking her **out of the picture** is the most important thing we can do."

You nod. "And if she's the boss, she's probably **right in the middle of the action**. It's probably a **safe bet** she's at the main exhibit right now."

Eric moves cautiously to the same door the guards entered through.

"Careful," you whisper.

"I don't hear anything," Eric reports back. He pushes the door wide open.

Your **jaw drops**. Standing in front of you is a large, beefy man dressed in black, his muscular arms crossed over his massive chest. You stare in disbelief as the giant glares back at you.

"*Excusez-moi!*" the man says, grabbing Eric by the shoulders. "Are you two really that incompetent? I can't believe you're both still in this area."

The man speaks English without any French accent. His voice is low and throaty, just like the voice you heard on the walkie-talkie.

"Uh . . ." Eric starts to say.

"Where are you two supposed to be right now?"

You and Eric look at each other, unsure.

"Main lobby?" you say, remembering the conversation earlier.

"Go!" the man booms.

Go to **page 115**.

Maddy seems like she is in control of the situation. So, you decide to **stay put** and **take your chances** with Willie.

"Come here," Willie yells, grabbing you roughly. He puts his arm around your neck. "We're going to have us some fun later," he whispers.

Maddy looks at you and then looks at Willie. "Don't hurt him," Maddy instructs Willie, much to your relief. She reaches out a hand and strokes your cheek. "I like this one."

"We have to go," Maddy's masked accomplice tells her.

"Alive, Willie," she warns him again.

Alone with Willie, you watch him pace back and forth, muttering to himself. "You? Why you?"

You try to stay very still.

"Okay, okay," he says, talking to himself. "I just won't hurt him that much. Not *too* much." Willie laughs maniacally, making you **jump**. "But only after we find a secret place to **put him away**."

Willie jabs his flashlight into your back, ordering you to walk ahead. You are directed to a small gallery filled with exhibits of old cookware and utensils.

Articles Ménagers

"Maddy told you not to hurt me," you remind Willie.

"She won't know," he says coldly. "I can't **let this go**. I can't have you going around telling people how you **got one over on me**."

Your **heart races**. "What if she finds out? You don't want to make Maddy angry now, do you?"

"Quiet!" he yells. Willie forces you to sit while he paces around.

"This exhibit makes me hungry," he continues on, mumbling to himself. Willie touches his nose and checks to see if he is still bleeding. "After we're done taking the painting, I'm going to have me a big meal. Maybe some French fries."

Is my fate really going to be decided by this psycho?

The man's mind seems to be unraveling by the minute. Seeing that Willie is distracted, you decide to **make a run for it**.

"Hey!" Willie shouts, **caught off guard**. He races after you.

You kick over a bench, knocking it into your captor's shins. When Willie continues to **charge at you**, you grab a plate from a display case and throw it at him. He blocks the plate with his arm, and it explodes into several fragments. You throw more plates.

Willie screams in pain as a few shards hit his face and eyes. "Rah!" he yells, **spitting out** a few pieces.

Taking another plate, you pretend to throw it. When Willie puts up his arms, you rush at him and smash the plate over his head. Plate after plate, you keep hitting him until he is **doubled over** on the floor, whimpering.

"You're dead," Willie whispers, his head and face bleeding.

You **whip around** and dash away to the next gallery.

Go to **page 120**.

"How could we?" you say. "You're so tall. Taller than the both of us, in fact."

From the **corner of your eye**, you can see Eric shake his head.

"What did you say?" Barrett roars. He reaches out and grabs you by the collar and **lifts you up**. "Do you think this is funny?"

"**Easy there**, big fella," Eric tells Barrett. "My friend was just trying to **lighten things up**."

"Shut up. How can you forget where you're supposed to be?"

You try to think of an answer, but your thoughts are focused on breathing as you feel Barrett's knuckles dig into your throat.

"Tell me!"

"What's . . . the question . . . again?" you ask through gasps of air.

Barrett looks at you with disgust. "You're definitely Willie's boys. He always picks the **bad apples**."

Eric tries to **calm down** Barrett, but it doesn't seem to work. "Just remind us, and we'll be **on our way**," Eric pleads.

Barrett drops you to the floor. "I'm going to ask you one more time," he says to you. "Depending on your answer, I'll decide whether you're worth **keeping around**, or whether I should leave you behind for the cops."

"We were helping with **clearing out** the crowds," you stammer. "But we heard there were a couple of tourists causing trouble. We came over here to help. When it was time to **meet up** with the rest of the group, we got confused and didn't get our new orders. We've been here in the bathrooms trying not to get in anyone's way."

Barrett huffs at your answer but seems to **buy it**. "Both of you are **a few cards short of a full deck**."

> If you decide to respond with, "We're not stupid. We're just confused," go to **page 119**.

> If you decide to respond with, "We don't think this is a game. We're being serious," go to **page 159**.

[CHAPTER THREE]

~Murphy's Law

YOU FOLLOW ERIC closely as you both walk away from the man.

"Hey! It's that way," the man yells, pointing to another door. "How stupid are you?"

"Right!" Eric says, **changing course**.

Soon, you find yourself back on the museum's main floor.

"I **need to go**," Eric says, **heading** toward the bathrooms.

You and Eric **take a moment** to relax near the sinks. The exhaustion and stress is finally **taking its toll**.

"This is crazy," you say out loud. You go and lean against one of the bathroom stalls. "My **head is spinning**." After **gathering your thoughts** and trying to **wrap your head around** what just happened, you notice that Eric is laughing.

"I can't believe we got out of that," he says, looking at you in the mirror. "Look," he says, showing you his hands. "I'm shaking."

"You're in shock. I think I'm going to **pass out**," you answer. "This was such a bad idea."

Eric's laughter **trails off**. "I'm actually starting to agree with you there. I've never been so afraid in my life. We're **in over our heads**. We should have left and found a way out and called the cops."

"The security guards are one thing. Huge bodybuilders who could crush our skulls—that's a **whole different ballgame**," you say.

"Aren't you glad we found these uniforms? They saved us."

"Someone in there?" a man calls from outside the bathroom entrance. You both freeze **in place** at the sound of the gruff voice.

Not again . . .

Before you can react, the door to the bathrooms opens slowly, and another large man enters—this one bigger than the last one. His eyes move quickly from Eric to you.

"What are you two doing in here?" he asks with a thick Australian accent.

With the best French accent you can fake, you answer, "We, uh, are waiting for the orders."

"*Oui*, waiting," Eric chimes in, pale with fear.

The enormous man sniffs and looks around the bathroom, inspecting it. He is dressed all in black and wears a thick, scruffy beard. To your horror, he puts a beefy hand on your shoulder.

"**Take it easy**. I'm just **crashing the party**. I'm **on a break** myself," the man says. With his left hand, he reaches into a pocket and **pulls out** a pack of cigarettes. He pounds the pack against his massive palm, and you flinch at the sound.

I definitely do not want to get into a fight with this man.

He holds the pack of cigarettes out to you, offering you a smoke. You shake your head, which is about all you can do right now because you are **tongue-tied** and completely **at a loss for words**. Eric, on the other hand, reaches out calmly from behind you and accepts one. After the man lights his cigarette, he offers the lighter to Eric who awkwardly takes it.

"Actually," Eric says, elongating the last syllable, "I will save mine for later." He winks. "For when we are celebrating our big prize."

The man scratches at his beard with his free hand and accepts the lighter back from Eric. He starts to chuckle. "What's with the fake French accents? You guys are terrible at it."

"Hah!" Eric grunts, pretending to be **in on the joke**. "We were just having a bit of fun."

To your horror, Eric has adopted an Australian accent now. *Idiot!* You glare at your friend who is nervously overacting.

"Are you Americans? Americans always **fall in love** with accents," the man says.

"**Nailed it!**" Eric says. "We are totally American."

"You must be Willie's recruits, eh?"

"Yup. You know Willie," Eric says. "He's hilarious."

"I'm Barrett," the Australian says, turning his eyes to you. "I'm the one giving orders when Maddy's too busy." He points at your jacket. "You boys can **take off** those fake uniforms now. The museum has been **cleared out**. It's just Maddy's crew and the people like you **in our pockets**."

Neither you nor Eric move. Though you have every intention of keeping the conversation going, you have no idea what to talk about.

Say something, stupid!

"Uh, yeah," you manage to say.

"Or you can keep them on," Barrett says, shrugging. "Whatever **floats your boat**."

The smell of cigarette smoke singes the insides of your nostrils. With each **drag**, the burly man doesn't puff as much as inhale the entire cigarette. You watch, hypnotized, as he **flicks the butt** into the sink. He **pulls out** another one from his pack. "A **second helping**," he says, **lighting up** and inhaling deeply. "Then it's back to the main exhibit."

"What's happening at the main exhibit?"

Barrett gives you a confused look. "The painting, mate."

"Right, right," you say, grimacing.

I can't believe I just said that . . .

You cough and **clear your throat**. "Um, how's that going by the way?" you continue.

"Could be better," Barrett says, looking at his feet. "Maddy's in a sour mood. I shouldn't be telling you this, but things aren't exactly going according to plan. **Murphy's Law**, I suppose."

"How so?"

"We knew what the security measures would be like here, but we underestimated how out-of-date the museum's systems would be. They must have put in some of these security gates recently without testing them, and the electronics are **acting up** all over the place. Amateurs. It's not the museums with the state-of-the-art security you have to worry about but the ones with the bad security."

"The fire alarms were going off all morning," Eric points out.

"Yeah," Barrett says, **rolling his eyes**. "**Tell me about it**. We couldn't get them going on time, and by the time we had things **in working order** we were **behind** an hour." Barrett **puts out** the second cigarette on the bathroom wall and flicks the butt into the sink. "An hour. In our **line of work**, that's an eternity."

"Crazy," Eric says. "Is there anything we can help out with?"

You give Eric a **dirty look**. He shrugs sheepishly.

Barrett chuckles. "Is Willie not working you hard enough? Don't you have your assignments already?"

"Um, well, we kind of forgot," Eric replies.

"Willie's instructions weren't very clear," you add quickly.

Barrett looks at the two of you and crosses his arms over his barrel-size chest. "You're joking, right?"

You both stand there, trying hard to **make eye contact** with the giant Aussie without flinching.

"Are you trying to **put one over on me**?" he demands.

If you decide to respond with, "How could we? You're so tall." go to **page 114**.

If you decide to respond with, "No. We just want you to explain the next step," go to **page 119**.

"We're just confused," you tell Barrett. "We just want you to explain the next step. My friend here was asking about the details earlier. He's not very **bright**."

Eric shrugs and slaps his forehead as if to emphasize your point.

"See? Definitely **a few cards short**," you add.

"I can see that, but I don't have time now," Barrett says, checking his watch. "Maddy's going to be **pissed off** at me for being gone too long. You boys, follow me. We'll **get you sorted**."

"How about we meet you there?" Eric interrupts. "I just need to use the toilet real fast." Eric retreats into a stall and unzips his pants.

Barrett's walkie-talkie emits a loud squeak. "I'm here," Barrett says into the receiver.

"Where are you?" a woman demands. "It's time to remove the package."

"On my way," Barrett says. "And I've got two of the recruits coming with me."

You give Barrett a weak **thumbs up**.

"Actually," he says. "I'll send these boys ahead. I forgot to give Francois something."

Barrett gives you his walkie-talkie, which has now gone silent. "I'm sending you idiots on ahead, but I need a favor."

"Anything," you say, swallowing hard.

"When you get to the main exhibit, go find Willie and give him this walkie-talkie. Tell him to get on the channel we talked about earlier."

And with that, Barrett leaves the bathrooms.

"You there, Eric?" you call out. "Are you alright?"

"Yeah," Eric says, flushing the toilet. "I almost **peed my pants**."

Go to **page 134**.

You grab a vase to use as a weapon against Willie. **Enough is enough.** This guy has been out there hunting you, and though you have felt helpless before, you are starting to feel like a caged animal ready to be **set free**. It is time to make sure this guy is **out of the picture**. You check the name of the gallery.

Poterie et Vases

The Pottery and Vases gallery. *My lucky day! Plenty of weapons here to choose from.*

You test the heaviest piece of pottery right next to you and **get a grip** on the handle. Too heavy. You **pick up** another vase, one that is much lighter but still hefty enough to break glass. You aim it at one of the frames on the wall across from you and hurl it through the air. The pottery hits the glass, shattering it to pieces.

Bull's eye! *That should get his attention.*

By the entrance, you **take apart** a trashcan and scatter the contents on the floor. Then you huddle in a corner and wait. The seconds **tick by** slowly, and doubt starts to **creep into your mind**. You **come to grips** with your situation. Should you just keep running instead of putting yourself in a defensive position by waiting? What do you know about dealing with art thieves—one, in particular, who seems to be a complete psycho?

But it is too late now. Moments later, Willie runs blindly into the gallery. As you hoped, he slips on the litter and slides across the glossy floor. He falls **flat on his back**. In seconds, you are on top of him, hitting him with a thick clay vase. As he tries to **get up**, you **connect with** his head. With the single blow, he **goes out like a light**.

You were lucky. That was a **close call**.

You flip him over and slip off his backpack. Rummaging through it, you find a length of rope and **tie him up**. Dragging him by his feet to the bathroom, you bind his limbs together and secure him to a toilet. You check the rest of his backpack and find a set of keys, a walkie-talkie, a large souvenir button, pens, and some paper with nothing written on them.

You grab the walkie-talkie and speak. "Hello? Maddy?"

"Who is this?" she snaps.

You are about to respond to her when someone else **cuts you off**.

"Attention, art thieves, attention. I'm **putting you on notice**! If you think you can just **waltz in here** and take a world-famous painting, **think again**. I'm going to hunt you down, one by one." There is a crackle over the channel. "And thank you for listening."

You stare at the walkie-talkie. The idiotic rant could only come from one person: Eric.

No one else is that brave. Or that stupid.

"Who was that?" someone asks.

"It's a tourist that's been giving us trouble in the administrative section," another person responds.

"**Take care of it**," Maddy commands.

Picturing Eric in your mind, you smile to yourself and shake your head. You have a lot of respect for your best friend, but his **big mouth** has always **found a way** to get him into trouble. You are also still worried about Darla. She could be anywhere, but you aren't safe on your own while Maddy and her friends are still in the area. If you could only get to Eric, you could **double your numbers**.

Go to **page 184**.

As quietly as you can, you drop your legs into the opening, feeling for a ladder rung. Your feet touch something solid and you begin climbing down into the darkness.

Red warning lights cast shadows on the tunnel walls. The air is musty, and the sound of electricity buzzes all around. Thick wires on the concrete walls **snake along** the length of the tunnel.

"Make sure you go down there and **pick up** anything we might have left behind," you hear from overhead.

"What?" the other person says. "Why don't you go down there?"

They begin to argue loudly.

I need to get out of here.

You **take off**. The tunnel echoes with the sound of your running footsteps as you race down the underground corridor. Your shallow breathing is the only other thing you can hear.

Up ahead, white lights dance. They lift, fall, and then suddenly **shoot back up** into the air. Your eyes follow their motion. A faint whizzing and cracking sound is made every time one of the lights pops. On closer look, you see that several of the electrical cables along the wall have been loosened and are now hanging freely. The clamps that once held the wires in place look like they have been broken off—and not **by accident**. The **live wires** aren't hanging low enough to reach you, but you might want to be careful as you **make your way** down the tunnel.

A set of tools stacked in a neat pile near the tunnel wall gets your attention. You **pick up** the pieces and examine the parts. There are pipes, duct tape, a drill set, and hammers. A box with digital timers and switches reveals what the culprits used to cause the damage to the wires. They must have built a small pipe bomb to bust the clamps off and split the wires.

As you walk further down the tunnel, you notice more wires snapping and sparking, this time with more intensity. Three wires thrash and shudder on the floor like snapping eels. You jump out of the way just as one wire whips at your ankles.

You go back to the tools. Digging through the discarded gear, you find a pile of coats. The coats are thick, and you wonder if they are heavy enough to drop onto the wires if they come near you.

You grab the coats and slowly **inch your way** back to the snaking, snapping electrical lines. You **duck under** a rogue wire that rattles against a harness. It loosens even more before snapping away. You see the first wire having spasms on the tunnel floor, and you float the coat on top of it. Though the sparking end furiously bounces along the concrete floor, the weight of the jacket keeps it from moving.

One down, two more to go.

The other two wires vibrate and hum, slicing the air with electric fury. You toss a coat in a desperate heave but miss. The remaining wires pop and snap angrily at you.

You are **down to** one coat and two wires now.

The last coat in hand, you wipe the sweat from your brow. Spreading it open in front of you, you take careful steps toward the loosened wires. If you can grab one of the wires from its base, you might be able to manage its movement. You know the risk, but you have no other choice.

You reach for it. The wire feels like a garden hose **out of control**, and it reacts angrily from being held. The loose end spins wildly in the air. With a twist of your body, you drop the last coat on top of it, holding it down.

With one last wire to go, you move to a safe distance. You stand back against the opposite wall and edge along sideways, watching the wire's movement. It whips back and forth erratically. You **wait for an opening** and then **take off** running. There is a snap right behind your ear as the electrified wire just misses striking your face.

At the end of the tunnel, you feel your neck and head. Drenched in sweat and shaking, you are amazed you **made it out** of there alive. You feel a little bit like Indiana Jones on his various adventures.

You remove your jacket and walk through a metal door **standing ajar**. The door leads to a small, rundown courtyard with a storage shed filled with construction tools. You are in an area outside of the museum that is under renovation. Overhead, scaffolding leads up to a door on the second floor. You climb it and eventually **make your way** through the door back inside the main building.

The first thing you notice is how dark it is inside. The emergency lights are very weak and don't reach many of the shadowy corners and alcoves. It is difficult to find your way around. Security gates have blocked several of the entrances to the galleries, limiting you to the main corridors and hallways. For a few more minutes, you walk around in a daze until you reach a staircase that goes to the second floor.

A bright light **spills through** a half-opened door. You hear a voice that sounds like Darla. You squint and climb the steps toward the landing to investigate. Just as you guessed, Darla comes running through the glass doors. Seeing you, she pauses before walking down to you.

"Darla!" you shout, meeting her **halfway up** the stairs.

"Sammy," she says, hugging you.

"I'm so glad to find you. I've been—"

"We have a problem," she says, interrupting you.

Your happy reunion is **cut short**. Scowling, Darla points at the glass doors from where she came through. Two men in museum guard uniforms walk out and stride toward you with menacing purpose.

"We're not alone."

Go to **page 36**.

Tobin is talking about escaping overseas—and possibly taking you with him.

"A getaway car, and then a getaway boat? That's insane," you say. "I don't think I can **get on board** with this plan. Take me by car—fine. That's it. No boats for me."

Tobin **bends down** to **wipe away** another spot of blood on the floor with his handkerchief. "I didn't say anything about using a boat to escape. I only meant that if I get caught, you get caught."

You are mildly relieved. "Of course," you say quickly, a little embarrassed. "I knew that. **We're in the same boat.**"

Tobin slaps you on the shoulder. "You're **one of us** now. Sort of."

Though you have no intention of joining this community of thieves, a part of you appreciates the idea of belonging to something. You have spent the entire day separated from your friends, and while you wished the circumstances were different, you feel a little pride knowing that Tobin considers you a part of his little gang.

"Fine. I'll **go along** with you," you say. "But there's a problem: You're the only one that considers me part of the crew."

"Of course," Tobin agrees. "You work for me. Consider it a subcontracting job."

"Wow, my first job," you say with a smirk. "Never considered thievery as a **line of work**."

You are being sarcastic, but Tobin **shrugs it off**. "I just need to know I can trust you," he replies. "To the police investigating this, you'll be as much a criminal as I am now, and you'll be **spending a lot of time** trying to convince them otherwise. Consider that fact if you ever get **second thoughts**. There's evidence."

"Got it. I just want to get out of here."

"Well, I have a plan," Tobin responds, sounding confident. He grins with pride.

"It looks like you do," you say.

Go to **page 100**.

Barrett takes you and Eric into the main exhibit. You are astonished at what you see and try to hide your shock. A crew is **hard at work** on removing the *Girl with a Pearl Earring* from its display.

It doesn't look easy though. Before they can get to the painting itself, they need to cut through the metal gate that has **closed down** around the exhibit. Only then can they **take apart** the protective metal case encircling the frame itself. Using power tools to cut the metal bars around the enclosure, the thieves make a tremendous amount of noise. The crew works steadily, **inch by inch**, severing each metal bar. Eventually, they will have access to the case itself.

"**Keep an eye on** this one, yeah?" Barrett says to one of his colleagues while pointing at Eric. Barrett **picks up** one of the cut bars and gives it to the man. "Hit him if he **tries anything**."

You feel a giant hand on your neck as Barrett pushes you forward. At the end of the room, you see Maddy impatiently giving orders through her walkie-talkie.

"Maddy," Barrett shouts, over the noise of the squealing saws. "Look what I found." He gives you a hard shove, and you almost fall right over. "This one **has a mouth on him**."

Maddy **takes one look** at you and drops her arm holding the walkie-talkie.

"Don't know where they found the guard uniforms," Barrett continues. "Almost fooled me until I **put two and two together**. They're not police, but they've been watching us."

Maddy's red lips form a sweet smile, but her green eyes look as piercing as ever. "We meet again," she says matter-of-factly. She gestures to Barrett without **taking her eyes off you**. "Help the others. My friend and I have some **catching up** to do."

The giant hand on your neck releases you, and Barrett walks over to assist the crew.

"Come now, say hello to an old friend," Maddy says, waving her clipboard and gesturing you over.

You back away as she approaches you.

"I'm truly hurt!" Maddy says, pretending to be offended. "You don't look very happy to see me. It's a reunion of old friends. Didn't we have such a great time together? Let's **bury the hatchet**."

"We are not friends," you say through gritted teeth.

"True," she admits. She sweeps her arm around the room. "But think of the irony, Sammy. We first met in this very room, and here we are again. Who knows? We might possibly be having our last conversation together."

You don't want to think about what she means by "last conversation" so you **put on** your bravest face. "You—you won't **get away** with this," you say, your **voice cracking** with fear anyway.

Maddy's **expression softens**, and she laughs. "I'll **give you credit**," she says. "You did make things difficult for us. But we improvised. All the **loose ends are being tied up** now—no thanks to you, of course. Now that you and your friend are **out of the way**, it should be **smooth sailing**."

"You sound like you've already **gotten away**. Sure about that?"

Maddy snorts. "I can't pretend as if this one's gone the way I wanted it to go. You wouldn't believe how many things have gone **belly up**. Believe me, not our usual style."

"I can believe it," you say, finding yourself agreeing with her. "This whole day's been one gigantic **snowball of a disaster**."

"That's exactly what I said!" Maddy exclaims, slapping her clipboard. "I said that to Francois, and he just looked at me like I was crazy. I really thought this small museum wouldn't be much of a challenge. I shouldn't have underestimated it. Oh, well. Lesson learned!"

You wonder how Maddy could be so casual about **ripping off** a museum. She shows no remorse or guilt.

"Why?" you ask her.

"Why what?" Maddy responds, looking confused.

"Why do you steal paintings?"

Maddy pauses to think of an answer. She scratches behind her ear while her green eyes shift left and right.

"Because it's fun," she tells you, shrugging. "Because it makes me rich."

"How noble of you."

She **leans in** close and looks directly at you—so close you can smell her perfume.

"And because it's the only thing I'm really good at."

"I guess that's as good as any reason for not **making an honest living**," you say dryly.

Maddy's face **turns dark**, and she drops the clipboard onto the floor as she raises her hands. "I'm so sick of people giving me that kind of **attitude**. I'm not some conflicted **cat burglar** with a **crisis of conscience**. I steal paintings. I'm good at it. Why should I stop?"

"We're through!" someone on power tool duty yells behind you. Maddy's crew cheers, and the men go to work on dropping the metal case surrounding the painting.

"**Easy as pie**," Maddy gloats, her eyes sparkling with pride.

"I guess you're right. You win, Maddy." Maybe a different approach will get you what you want. "So, why keep hostages? Let me and my friends go. We'll just **move on** and get out of here. We'll return home with a crazy story about a brilliant mastermind who **pulled the wool over everyone's eyes**."

Maddy looks at you and considers your suggestion for a moment. You are hopeful.

"No," Maddy says finally. "I can't risk letting you all out onto the street, screaming about the art robbery."

"You'd rather **hand us over** to the police? We'll be witnesses," you reason. "Let us go now. **No hard feelings**. Can't you see? You've won. The painting is all yours. Or it will be soon enough."

Maddy taps her cheek, and she **looks down her nose** at you. "It would be nice to have someone **spread the word** about Madeleine de Castellano."

You keep going. You hope that appealing to Maddy's inflated ego will override her **common sense**. "Yes!" you say excitedly. "You'll be a legend. Think of it as the ultimate souvenir. You're letting me and my friends go with a memory we can share with others—with the world!"

"How can I trust you?"

"How can you not? Even if we called the police, you'll all **be long gone** by then. I'm sure you have a **surefire way** out, don't you?"

This last question annoys Maddy. "Of course! Look around," she says. "Does this look like a **two-bit operation**? You're looking at a crime scene that will be studied for years. Books will be written about it." Maddy **picks up** her clipboard and begins to scribble notes. "Maybe that'll be my next **pet project**," she ponders out loud.

"Clear!" someone shouts.

Maddy walks past you to inspect the crew's work. The thieves have gone from power tools to large circular magnets that have been attached around the protective metal case.

Maddy sees you staring in awe and explains. "There's no cutting involved at this stage. The locks inside the protective case need to be pulled. We're using magnets to move the parts inside." She fans herself. "Ingenious, right?"

It is only a **matter of time** before Maddy and her gang reach the painting, and then the *Girl with a Pearl Earring* will be **gone for good**. You think about Darla and her deep affection for the portrait. The work never really impressed you, but you know that it has millions of fans around the world. It would be a shame to see it disappear, to be **sold on the black market** to some private collector. You turn to Maddy and make one last appeal.

"Don't do it, Maddy," you say. "Please don't take the painting."

"What?"

"It's not too late. It's a masterpiece. You're not just stealing it from the museum. You're stealing it from the world."

She snorts. "You art lovers. All so sentimental." Maddy snaps her fingers at someone behind you. "Francois, take him," she instructs.

The man grabs you and leads you out of the main exhibit hall into another gallery.

"Where are you taking me?" you demand.

"Sit on that bench," your captor instructs, rummaging through a bag. He takes out a clump of zip ties and orders you to put your hands behind your back.

"And if I don't?"

"I will **make you**," Francois responds.

You start to back away from him. You keep moving until your back **presses up** against a glass display.

"Come back here," the man orders. "I don't understand why you hostages never listen."

You put your hands behind your back. The man spins you around. He starts to put the zip tie around your wrists, but you keep spinning. The zip tie falls.

"Stop moving!" Francois says, trying to keep you still.

You **whip around** again, this time pushing the man hard into a glass display. The shelves **break apart**, and the heavy artifacts on them **come crashing down** on his head.

Go to **page 194**.

You need to be more cautious and consider your options more carefully. You feel less comfortable with the thought of having to risk your life in an unnecessary **death match** with Maddy's craziest goon. If you can **stay one step ahead** of your attacker, you will be safe. If you get caught, you will have no choice but to **stand your ground**.

You stay low, crawling **on your hands and knees**, moving from table to table, and display case to display case. In the silence, you feel a little bit of comfort. You hope it will last.

How did it get to this?

More than anything, all you want to do now is to get out of this museum and get on a plane with Eric and go home. But what about Darla? You have no idea where the thieves have taken your friend. She might be **tied up** somewhere, held as a hostage. You want to find her and make sure she is safe, but how? The last time you saw her was near the stairs where you were separated.

You walk into the nearby bathrooms to **gather your thoughts**. Finding a map in the trash, you study it until you know the building's layout like the **back of your hand**.

Then you decide: *Darla, I'm coming for you.*

Go to **page 207**.

Tobin is saying you are now in the same situation as he is. He is right. He has your fingerprints on the same tools the thieves have used.

Fine. Let him believe I'm an accomplice now.

This might be the best way to gain Tobin's trust and protect yourself, even if it means working with a criminal. "The **same boat**," you **parrot back** to Tobin, offering your hand. "I'm trusting you to get me out of here safely."

Tobin shakes your hand. "Okay," he says energetically.

You think about what it means to have your fingerprints on the tools and decide nothing will stop you from trying to save Darla and Eric. If Tobin knew you had everything to lose by leaving France without your friends, he might resort to more extreme and meaningful threats to keep you away from the police. For now, you just have to **play along** and let Tobin believe you **pose no threat**.

"When we **take out** Frankie, he'll **think twice** about ever messing with me again. **Brains over brawn**, right?"

"Take out Frankie?" you ask. "You said no killing."

"Of course! No killing! You'll go into one car. When Frankie gets into the driver's seat of your car, you'll hit him on the head. After that, I'll have the car stop somewhere safe, so you can leave. The police will find an unconscious Frankie along with some stolen goods. I'm **setting him up** to **take the fall**. That's how I'll take him out."

"Um, I'm supposed to **knock out** Frankie? With what?"

"I don't know," Tobin says, waving the thought away. "**Keep an eye out** for something you can use on the ogre."

You start to wonder if Tobin is as smart as he thinks he is. He might have some **bright ideas**, but you understand how someone like Frankie could get angry with him.

"Brains over brawn," you remind Tobin. "I think we need a smarter plan—one that involves less, uh, head bashing."

Tobin's eyes **light up**. "I just thought of something!"

Go to **page 100**.

Tobin means you should do what is expected of you and follow the original plan. You nod reluctantly and follow him. "Let's **deliver the goods**," you repeat. "Let's get this done."

Tobin stops you as you near a car in the parking garage. "Hold on," he says, **taking a deep breath**. "I need to prepare myself. I'm a **bundle of nerves** right now."

"You steal paintings **for a living**, and this makes you nervous?"

"There's **no telling** what Frankie will do if he catches you or **finds out** what I'm doing. Of course I'm nervous!"

Tobin shakes his head, **cracks his knuckles**, and stretches his arms. Eventually, he **pulls out** a tablet from his pack.

"It's going to **take me a while** to **run this program** though. I'll have to tweak the code . . . So, you'll have to **take watch**. Whistle if anyone comes."

"Sounds **easy enough**," you say. You jog behind a large van, drop to the floor, and roll underneath it, between the tires. You **keep an eye out** for any unexpected visitors.

"If he sees you, run," Tobin warns.

You give him a doubtful look.

"You'd be surprised. He's pretty **quick on his feet**."

"Anything else I need to know?"

"Frankie likes to inflict pain," Tobin says matter-of-factly.

You **eye** Tobin warily. "Well, *that* I already knew."

Tobin's tablet chimes. "Okay, we're good," he says.

He walks over to the driver's side of the car and opens the door. He turns to you and **makes a show** of pressing the tablet with his forefinger. The car suddenly **turns on** and revs its engine with a loud *vroom*. He taps the tablet again, and the car **shuts off**.

"It works! One more, and then we can get to the loading zone."

Go to **page 135**.

You inspect the walkie-talkie, flipping it around in your hands. There is a button for talking, a digital display showing the frequency and channel, and a couple of knobs for volume. You think about who would be listening on their walkie-talkies. You imagine **reaching out** to Maddy. What would you even say to her?

"Maddy, leave the painting. You don't have to do this."

The exhaustion from lack of sleep and the stress of the day is **wearing you down**. You feel ready to collapse. Eric takes the walkie-talkie from you and puts it into his pocket.

"Let's get out of here," he says. "We have a delivery to make."

You look down at your hands. They are shaking uncontrollably. You sway on your feet.

"Are you all right?" Eric asks.

You go limp for a quick second, and then your body jerks awake.

"**Wake up**," you hear Eric saying to you.

"Um, why am I wet?" you ask. For some reason, your face is drenched in water.

"I splashed water on you. I didn't know how else to wake you."

"I **blacked out**?"

"Easy, buddy," Eric replies.

He helps you up, and your knees begin to **fold again**. You lean against the sink and gulp water from the tap.

"We don't have to **keep going**, you know," Eric says to you.

"We need to stop them," you say, feeling delirious now. "It's our mission now." You stumble out of the bathrooms in a daze.

"You don't look so good. You sure you're **cut out for this**?" Eric asks you.

> If you think that Eric is saying you should leave the museum, go to **page 155**.

> If you think that Eric is asking whether you are capable of finishing the mission, go to **page 160**.

You walk with Tobin and go another level down in the parking garage. "Maddy's getaway is the most important phase in her schemes," Tobin explains to you. "Once the **package**—the painting or whatever—is **in her hands**, we escape to the designated exit routes. Our job as her crew is to make sure the exits are **free and clear**. We always plan several routes. Plan A, B, and so on. In this museum, all our routes **lead** to this place."

"Lead to what?" you ask, looking around.

Tobin coughs and points to a sports car with a bright red **paint job**. The car looks incredibly expensive and fast.

"No way," you say **under your breath**.

"Maddy loves red," Tobin says. "She'll want this car." As Tobin works on another tablet to **take control** of the sports car, he orders you to **stand guard** and **keep your eyes open**.

"We're **in the home stretch**," Tobin tells you, "but we can't get comfortable yet."

"Seems like a bad choice though," you tell Tobin. "It's pretty, but it doesn't look like it can fit a lot of loot."

"All Maddy cares about is the **big prize**. She'll take the *Girl with a Pearl Earring* and sell it. We all **get a cut**, of course, but me and the guys make most of our money selling whatever else we steal."

You **keep watch**, looking for **any sign** of movement. It seems **like an eternity** as Tobin **hacks his way** into the system of the sports car. "The software runs bits of code over a wireless network into a receiver I installed into the OBD-II port. With a virus embedded into an MP3, I can send commands through the telematics system."

"Um, in English please?" you say.

Tobin laughs. "Basically, it works. You'd be surprised to know how much software controls even the little things on a car." Tobin points to the car's front wheels, which slowly begin to turn as he taps the tablet's touchscreen. "Everything from the windshield wipers to the radio station on the stereo unit."

Tobin walks to the passenger-side door and opens it. "Get in," he says with a grin, pointing at the driver-side door. "Let's **test this out**."

You lift the lever but nothing happens.

"Sorry," Tobin says, looking down at his tablet. You hear the click of the car door's lock. "Try it now."

You take a seat inside the fancy sports car. The dashboard looks like something you might find in a jet cockpit. The car's engine **roars to life** as Tobin starts the car with his tablet.

"Go on. **Take the wheel**," he tells you. "**Give it a whirl**."

You **step on the gas**, and the car lurches forward.

"Never been in a car like this before, eh?"

You shake your head wordlessly.

"Just **take it slow**."

"**Here goes**." You drive steadily through the parking garage until you reach the ground level. Two guards stop you near the exit.

"Hey, it's me," Tobin says, **sticking his head out** the window.

"Tobin, Frankie is looking for you," one guard says sternly.

"Frankie? What does he want?"

"He's gone inside the museum for now, but he wants to discuss something with you as soon as possible."

"What?" Tobin says, surprised. "We're **in charge** of getting the cars ready!"

"Sorry. **Change of plan**. You are to stay here with us."

"I don't understand," Tobin says. His face pales with worry.

The guard standing near your window looks at you suspiciously.

"He's **with me**," Tobin tells him.

"**Nice ride**," the guard near you comments.

"It's Maddy's," you respond.

The guard speaking to Tobin **clears his throat**. "Frankie said you haven't been doing your job, Tobin." The guard turns to you. "Please park the car here and get out."

"No," Tobin says. "I work for Maddy directly. You guys answer to me."

"We're doing what Frankie has ordered," the guard says, trying to open the driver's door. He looks confused when it doesn't budge.

"Listen," Tobin says, **thinking on his feet**. "Let's get this all **straightened out**. Frankie's upset about something, and all we have to do is talk to him. Yes, sometimes we **don't see eye to eye**. Frankie has a temper. He gets angry. But he's a reasonable man."

"Are you sure you are talking about the same Frankie? I think you have him **pegged wrong**."

Tobin tries a different tactic. "Fine. How about you let my friend and me finish packing the vehicle, and maybe I **slip you** a few items in another car."

The guards look at each other and smile uneasily.

"**Do we have a deal**?"

"That sounds like something we can surely **work with**," the guard closest to Tobin says. "But maybe you can **sweeten the deal** for us."

"What else do you guys want?" Tobin asks.

The other guard near you starts to look uncomfortable with the offer. He begins to converse with the other guard in French. It sounds like an argument is **breaking out**.

"What's the problem now?" Tobin asks.

The guard speaking to Tobin explains. "My friend here is worried that Maddy will be furious if she ever finds out about this secret arrangement with you. She may decide to **cut us out** of the profits. We need more assurances."

"I'll speak to her directly," Tobin says. "**Don't sweat it**. And you've got plenty of **other chips to cash in** to **make up** for any lost rewards."

The nervous guard scoffs. "If you were Frankie, I would believe you. But you are no Frankie."

Tobin's face **turns bright red**. "I'm a part of Maddy's crew too."

"*Oui*. But you are Tobin," the guard says with a shrug. "You are just—how you do you say—a **grunt**."

The guard knocks on your car door and directs you to get out. You look back at Tobin, waiting for some kind of signal. You can tell the **wheels are turning in his head.**

What is he thinking?

"Listen closely," Tobin says. "We'll have to **cut to the chase.**"

If you think that Tobin is telling you to drive the car through the gate and start a chase, go to **page 139.**

If you think that Tobin is telling the guards he wants to be honest and give them a direct, straightforward answer, go to **page 145.**

Tobin is telling you to drive the car through the gate and start a chase. Without thinking, you **step on the gas** hard. The engine **revs up**, and the car crashes through the gate, nearly hitting the guard.

"What are you doing?" Tobin cries.

"**Cutting to the chase**," you reply. "Doing what you said."

"**Are you nuts**? That's not what I meant!"

The car skids onto the street, barely missing oncoming traffic. Tobin howls in terror. Car horns come in all directions as you swerve between other vehicles and veer from lane to lane. You struggle with the steering wheel.

"We're going too fast!" you shout. "I can't control the car. It's not responding."

"**Watch out!**" Tobin screams.

With a jerk of your arm, you swerve out of the way of another car. You have dodged a serious collision, but the car still smashes into you from behind. The **world spins**. All you can hear is the screech of the tires and a loud, metallic crunch.

"Are you okay?" you ask Tobin after the car **comes to a stop** at the side of the road.

Tobin groans, holding his arm close to his side. "I think it's broken," he says, grimacing.

The car's airbags have deployed, and the smoke from the engines makes it hard to see and breathe. You open the door and fall out onto the street. A crowd gathers around you. The smell of burnt rubber fills the air. On the road behind you, you see trails of crazy skid marks on the asphalt.

Security guards near the museum entrance recognize Tobin and rush to help him get out of the car. One of them takes you by the arm and leads you back to the museum.

"No," you tell him weakly. "Let me go. I need to get away from here." You **double over**, dizzy and nauseated.

"They have seen you!" the guard says, genuinely concerned. "We must hide you inside."

He must think you are one of Maddy's crew.

"What were you doing out there on the street?"

"A little **joyriding**," Tobin says bitterly.

"We must go tell Maddy what has happened," the guard says.

"Oh, no. **We're done**," Tobin tells you with a groan.

As the two guards drag you away from the wreckage and back to the museum, you try to resist.

"Don't bother, Sammy," Tobin says. He seems **resigned to his fate**. "We're so done. **Toast**."

Toast. It is the last thing you hear before you lose consciousness.

Go to **page 182**.

Eric means you need to perfect a plan first. "Okay," you say, agreeing. "Let's **figure out** something before we try to **save the day**. The security station—" You stop talking when you feel your head swoon. "Sorry. **Head rush.**"

"Are you all right?" Eric asks.

"I'm actually feeling pretty tired now," you admit. "I was saying that the security station would be a good place to **hammer out a plan**."

When you reach the security station, Eric **heads over** to a small kitchen where he finds a coffee pot filled with water. "Drink," he says, offering you a mug. Lukewarm water **never tasted so good**.

"I was just faking being tired," you say.

"Now *that* I don't believe," Eric says, before gulping down some water with you.

The security room is divided into two sections. You see a meeting room area filled with tables and chairs. There are rows of lockers on one side. This must be where the security guards **take their breaks** and wait for assignments. At the far end, you see a small glass enclosure filled with monitors and terminals. That must be where they **keep an eye** on everything happening inside the museum.

You **walk up** to the glass enclosure and press your face against the surface and peer inside. There is a long console of blinking lights under a row of monitors hanging from the ceiling. The door is half open, so you walk right in. All of the monitors are switched on, but the words "No Signal" flash on the screens.

"Look at that," Eric says, pointing at some wires. Unconnected power cords and cables are left splayed where a computer must have been. "Looks like paintings aren't the only things they're stealing."

"Must be security footage," you tell Eric. "These cables must have connected to a computer or recording device."

"What about this?" Eric asks, holding up smashed bits of a digital recording machine. "Here's the hammer they used."

"**Covering their tracks.** So much for the evidence. If only we could get the monitors working again. Any ideas?"

"**Your guess is as good as mine,**" Eric says.

He considers the panels for a moment before slamming his palm onto the various buttons on the console.

"Dude, what are you doing?"

Red lights turn green, and **vice versa,** as the entire console begins to hum and buzz. Several of the screens begin to blink with a signal.

"Well, now it's working," Eric says.

You point at one of the monitors. "There!" You recognize the area where you first lost your tour group. "That's where I was standing when I saw you guys at the main exhibit."

"Great," Eric says. "That tells us where that camera is. Now, how do we change views?"

Suddenly, the walkie-talkie in Eric's pocket buzzes. "Who's messing with the security gates?" someone asks.

"We sure got their attention," you say. You scan the monitors and see that the security gates at a gallery are slowly lowering down. "You must have triggered some of the security measures," you say.

"Answer them," Eric says, holding the walkie-talkie to you.

You press the talk button. "Uh, we're just having some technical difficulties."

"I'm **on my way,**" a voice responds.

Eric groans. "We're going to **have some company.**"

You stare at the monitors and see someone moving stealthily from under an open security gate in one of the other galleries. It doesn't look like anyone on Maddy's crew.

"Who is that? Can we **zoom in?**"

"Try this," Eric says, moving a control stick under the monitor.

The camera **zooms in** on a familiar face.

"Darla!" you and Eric say at the same time.

"What is she doing?"

On the screen, Darla stops, her back pressed tensely against a wall. Her face is **filled with fear**, and she **stares off into the distance**. From one corner, a shadowy figure approaches. Slowly, Darla lifts a vase and hurls it at the person. Before that person can recover, Darla **dashes off** into another gallery.

"Did you see that?" Eric shouts.

You have to **figure out** how to help Darla. "**Keep an eye on** that screen," you tell Eric. "Tell me if you see anything change."

You press random buttons and wait for Eric to say something.

"You just changed the view on the monitor," he says. You **make a mental note**.

"How about now?" you ask, pressing more buttons.

"It looks like you're switching to different cameras in that area. I just saw Darla running through another gallery."

"Each of these monitors must be connected to a set of cameras." Your hand hovers over another set of buttons.

"That monitor!" Eric says, pointing. "The gates. Look! They're going up."

"And now?" you ask.

"Going down. Looks like you're **figuring this out**," Eric observes. He watches your fingers and **looks up** at the monitors. "I think we have this console **figured out**." Eric takes the controls.

"What are you doing?"

"Go get Darla," he instructs. "I'll **keep track** of you on the monitors to lower and raise the gates." Eric **tests out** several of the buttons, and some of the monitors **flicker on**. "I think I **got the hang of this**."

"And what about you?" you ask. "One of those thieves will be here **any minute now**."

"Don't worry about me," Eric replies. "Darla needs your help. I can just lock myself in this room." Eric goes to the door and slides the hammer through the handles. "See?" he says.

"Okay." The barrier is crude but effective.

"Take this," Eric says, handing you a walkie-talkie that he **picks up** from a charger.

You walk out of the room, and Eric **bars** the door again with the hammer. For **good measure**, he jams a chair up against the glass for extra support. You kick the door to test it. Eric gives you a **thumbs up**. Before you go, Eric waves at you and points to the walkie-talkie in his hand, showing you a frequency and channel. You turn the dials until you hear his voice.

"Can you hear me?"

"**Loud and clear**," you say into the receiver.

"Good. I'll lead you as long as I can."

You **take off**. In the distance, you hear footsteps and duck into a side room. Eric's voice crackles on the walkie-talkie. "I think Darla's somewhere on the second floor. There are a lot of ancient artifacts, like vases and decorations."

"I know where that is," you say, remembering the details of the map you studied.

The walkie-talkie hisses and crackles. From your crouched position, you can see several men running in the direction of the security room.

"Eric, I hate to tell you this, but **you have guests**," you tell him.

"How many?" he asks.

"Hard to tell. A few. Should I come back?" you ask.

"No. Just find Darla and get out of the museum. Call for help! I'll **hold down the fort**."

All of a sudden, the walkie-talkie **goes dead**.

If you decide to return and help Eric, go to **page 162**.

If you decide to leave and go find Darla, go to **page 165**.

Tobin is telling the guards he wants to be honest and give them a direct, straightforward answer. If they think he is sincere, they might let you pass through. Although the guards look **hard to please**, they also seem eager to hear what Tobin has to say. You hope he gives them a deal they would be foolish to **pass up**.

"I'll **cut to the chase**," Tobin repeats. "We don't have a lot of time, and we have several cars downstairs that are going to be filled with tons of stolen artwork soon. I'll give you a programmed tablet for the green van back there. All you have to do is let us go, and you can start **playing around** with the controls. I'd advise one of you to stay here and make sure no one else enters the parking garage."

The guards look at each other and begin to discuss Tobin's proposal in French. Then they turn back to him. "Would you say this van is **worth our cut** in the painting?" one of the guards asks.

"Definitely," Tobin says. "**Between you and me**, it's not going to be an issue. Maddy could **care less** about what you guards **take on the side**."

"Gerard will go and check this green van. If the computer does not work, he will come looking for you. Please drive around and park by the green van."

"Fine," Tobin says, shrugging. "I'd offer Gerard a ride, but this car only seats two."

"*Au revoir*," the guard says, before **waving you off**.

"Sammy, get ready to **punch it**," Tobin whispers to you as the one guard begins to walk toward the van.

"Excuse me?" you say.

"We can't stay here. I can't stay here. There was no way Maddy, let alone Frankie, would be okay with these guards grabbing some of the loot. I **made that up**! I had to pretend to **get them out of our hair**."

"What are you saying?" you ask.

"I'm saying I **screwed up**. This is getting **way out of hand**. The plan is **finished**. You have to drive us out of here and fast!"

The other guard goes back to the booth. You **press the gas** with your foot several times, and the car jerks forward.

"I'm **taking over**," Tobin says, panicking. Suddenly, the car begins to roll. "We're **out of here**!"

Exploding ahead, the car crashes through the barrier.

You look in the rearview mirror. "He's on his walkie-talkie," you tell Tobin.

The car steers through oncoming traffic before it settles into a steady cruise. Your **heart beats wildly** in your chest. "What do we do now?" you yell.

"I'll **drop you off** near those shops."

"And what about you?"

"I'll **disappear** for as long as I can," Tobin replies. "For now, I'm **home free**. By the time they get the painting and come looking for me, I'll be **long gone**."

The car stops near a row of shops as Tobin slides down in his seat **out of view**.

You sit there, unmoving. Something in Tobin's pocket beeps. The walkie-talkie. Chaotic chatter comes from the walkie-talkie, and you can barely **make out** the words.

"Great," Tobin says. "They're looking for us now. Let's go!"

You hesitate, **listening in** on the conversation. "What was that?" you ask. "What did that last person say?"

Tobin puts the walkie-talkie to his ear. "Sounds like they're **rounding up** the hostages. They know that we've escaped. Now they're going to create a situation to keep the police from **storming** the museum."

"Oh, no," you say with a **sinking feeling**. "What did we do?"

"Don't worry. Maddy won't harm the hostages."

"You sure about that?"

Tobin shrugs. "Well, maybe. It's not like this has never happened. In case the police ever get called or there's a situation, the hostages are **rounded up** and used as **bargaining chips**."

"Bargaining chips?"

"Yeah, we tell the cops to let us go, or we say we'll kill all the hostages. The threats usually work."

Your eyes grow wide.

"They don't mean it. They just say that."

"I have to go back," you tell Tobin. "I have friends who were in the museum, and I don't want to be the reason they get hurt."

Tobin **rolls his eyes**. "Friends? Why didn't you mention friends before? Your *friends* were probably evacuated. The only hostages we have are the security guards who didn't want to join our operation and some tourists like you who didn't leave when they should have."

You shake your head. "I have to go back," you tell Tobin. "I have to make sure my friends are okay."

"Well, don't you have a cellphone or something?" he asks. Your hands instinctively check your pockets, and you remember you lost your phone and wallet.

"Just take me to the front of the museum," you tell Tobin. "I need to know they're safe."

"Fine," Tobin says, **turning the car around**. "But if you really care about the hostages, you won't call the cops anytime soon. If Maddy knows the police are out there or **on their way**, things will get complicated. Best thing to do is to let this **take its course**."

You agree. Tobin steers the car back to the museum and **drops you off**.

"Thanks," you say as you get out of the vehicle. Before you **run off**, Tobin signals for you to wait. He tosses you the walkie-talkie and forces a smile.

"Go find your friends," he says. "And some free advice: Pretend you're part of the crew. Use the walkie-talkie. Find out if any of the hostages look like your friends."

"Okay."

"Good luck."

Before you can say anything else, Tobin and the car **speed off**.

Security guards have formed a barricade around the main entrance of the museum to make sure all visitors stay out. You wander toward the front of the crowd.

"The situation is **under control**," one of the guards keeps saying to reassure some upset tourists. "But you must be patient. When we have **figured out** the problem, we will let you back in to get whatever you have left behind."

"What about our cars?" a tourist asks.

"Like the museum, the parking garage will be opened as soon as the situation is **sorted out**," the guard replies.

You feel bad for the visitors whose cars are being stolen, and you consider telling everyone about the real situation happening in the museum. But you decide not to spread panic and worry. Tobin is right. The **best course** is to let the robbery happen. In the meantime, you have to adapt and **roll with the punches**.

You search the **faces in the crowd** but find **no sign** of Darla and Eric. You do find your tour guide from earlier.

"There you are!" she yells, grabbing your arm.

"Do you know where my friends are?" you ask her.

She shakes her head. "I haven't been able to find them since we were evacuated."

"They must still be inside."

"I don't know. Everyone is **accounted for** except for them." She points at the other members of your tour group.

You walk away and **take out** the walkie-talkie Tobin gave you. You find a quiet place away from the crowd and think about what you will say. You practice your French accent, but it sounds terrible. You **throw caution to the wind** and press the talk button.

*It's **now or never**.*

"Hostages," you say. "How many do we have?" The walkie-talkie beeps. You hear someone breathing loudly over the channel.

"Ten to twelve," a deep voice responds. **"Give or take."**

"Do we have any of their names?" you ask. You regret the

question immediately. Is name-taking something criminals do when they take hostages?

"No, we don't have their names," someone answers. "Why?"

"I'm looking for someone," you say. "An Eric or a Darla." You know the request is a **shot in the dark**, but you are desperate.

"Darla? Yeah, I have a Darla," a different voice says, sounding bitter. "She's a little firecracker. The troublemaker bit me on the hand while I was trying to **tie her up**. If you all bothered to grab their wallets and purses, you'd know who was who."

Should I call the police?

You walk over to someone in the crowd. "May I use your cellphone?" you ask.

"For what?" the woman asks.

"I need to call for help. Something's happening inside the museum," you say.

"What's happening?"

She looks at you suspiciously. She speaks in a foreign language to a companion, and they both stare at you oddly. You back away slowly. You remember Tobin's warning and start to regret what you revealed. Watching your expression change, the woman begins to panic. She says something to her other companions, and the group starts arguing.

"No, no. Forget I said anything," you say, realizing how out of control things are getting already. You pretend to laugh. "I was just kidding. A joke!"

Going back in alone seems like your only option. But how will you **make it** past all the security?

You walk around, looking for an area near the entrance where there are fewer guards. One section of the museum undergoing construction has only one guard posted in front of it. This could be your only chance to get in.

When a man talking loudly on his cellphone walks in front of you, you grab the phone out of his hands. You run to a guard, tossing him the device and **take off** running. As the confused man goes to get his phone from the equally confused guard, you **disappear into the crowd**. More guards and curious tourists gather around the man and guard. You **wind your way** back to the section **closed off** by tape and orange construction cones. The open area undergoing renovation is empty, and you slip easily under the tape and signs.

Scaffolding, like a series of ladders and ledges, leans against the building. It looks sturdy enough, so you start to climb until you find a ledge that leads to an open window.

You step through the window into a darkened room lit by natural light coming through an opening in the roof. Heavy rolls of cloth are strewn about. Buckets of paint are stacked in a corner alongside piles of wood and other construction materials. Near some of the supplies, you find a lukewarm coffee mug sitting next to a security guard's jacket. Someone must have been on guard duty here, but the person seems to have **moved on** to something else.

You fooled the guards earlier into thinking you were Tobin's associate. Maybe you can **keep up the act** by **putting on** the guard's jacket. As you **slip it on**, the walkie-talkie in your pocket buzzes and beeps. In the **dead silence**, it sounds deafening.

You **take a deep breath** and press the talk button. "Hostage check. I need the location of a Darla," you say. "Repeat: Darla."

"East Wing. Who's this?"

You decide to leave that question unanswered. You look around and **get your bearings**, unsure about which direction to go. There is the East Wing with Darla, of course, but there is also the rest of the museum to investigate.

> If you want to investigate the area more and decide on a plan later, go to **page 151**.

> If you want to go to the East Wing now, go to **page 192**.

You want to investigate the area more and decide on a plan later. While you want nothing better than to **charge to the rescue** of your friends, it would be best to **scope out** the rest of the museum to see what you might be **up against**.

***Hang in there**, Darla.*

Quietly, you leave the construction area to go inside the museum. You are on the second floor, judging by the signs around you. You **make a mental list** of what you know and the dangers you could expect: Maddy is stealing the *Girl with a Pearl Earring*. Darla is somewhere in the East Wing, being **held against her will**. Tobin is long gone. And where's Eric?

The signs up ahead indicate that the main exhibit is nearby. The only way to know **for sure** how close Maddy is to stealing the famous painting is by seeing her progress **in person**.

As you **make your way** back to the main exhibit, you keep alert, following the signs and making sure nothing **jumps out** at you from the darkness. Maddy's crew or the hostages are nowhere to be seen, but your **ears perk up** whenever a sound echoes through the empty hallways and galleries. Security gates at the entryways to the galleries turn sections into long and dangerous corridors. There are only a few places to hide. If someone were to approach you from ahead or behind, you would only have one other direction to go.

As you approach the main exhibit, you begin to hear voices and what sounds like construction noise. A security gate blocks your way forward, so you look for another route. Then you see it: A gate left partially open at a small gallery off to the side allows you passage. The thieves have inadvertently created a maze by leaving some galleries accessible while blocking off others completely.

You eventually reach another **dead end**. A security gate blocks the way to the main exhibit, and there is **no other way around it**. Hoping to find something that might help you pry open the gate, you **take a look around**. From the **corner of your eye**, you see something move. A security camera on the ceiling swivels from side to side, scanning the room. As calmly as you can, you walk away from the camera's **line of sight** and **keep clear** of its view. If Maddy's crew is watching, you hope they mistake you for one of their guards.

Nearby, a grinding mechanical noise **catches your attention**. To your shock, you see one of the security gates near you lifting off the floor.

Someone must have spotted me on the cameras.

Do they want to let you in, or are they sending someone after you? You wait for footsteps, but when you hear nothing, you drop to your hands and knees and crawl under the gate. Up ahead, another gate lifts to let you through. Someone is definitely leading you toward the main exhibit. Your body begins to shake with nervousness, but you **push forward**.

You can now see the gallery with the main exhibit. At the entrance to the room, a security gate blocks the way, but you are close enough to see several of Maddy's men **hard at work** at the far end of the room. You wish **you could tell** how close they are to stealing the painting.

"*Etes-vous une pause?*" a voice says.

Startled, you look up and see a security guard who has come in from a side door.

"Uh, no? *Non*," you say awkwardly.

The guard shifts to English. "You must be one of Maddy's."

"Yes," you say curtly. "That's exactly what I am."

The guard **raises an eyebrow**. You want to **kick yourself** for sounding so forced.

"Well, they are almost finished," the guard observes. "Then, **jackpot**. We win."

"I hope so," you say. "I **can't wait** for this to be finished."

"Let us go watch them, no?" he says.

"Go on ahead," you tell him. "I, uh, want to **take a look** around. It's not often you get a whole museum **all to yourself**."

The guard's walkie-talkie beeps. Maddy is giving orders. "I need a **few more hands** at the main exhibit," she says. "Everyone in the garage, set your clocks for five minutes. In ten minutes, all personnel can leave the building. Soon enough, we'll all be a little richer."

"You heard her," the guard says. "Sightseeing is over. We must hurry and join the others."

You could try to **fight off** the guard, but it would **raise suspicion**. A few other crew members and guards are entering the room from the side door now, and you realize you have no choice but to follow him as he greets the rest of the group.

You nearly **trip on your feet** when you see Frankie.

Frankie strolls to the far corner of the room and **sits down** for a cigarette break. The group walks in that direction, and soon you are a few feet away from him. You turn away, hoping he won't notice you.

To your horror, you feel his hand **slap down** on your shoulder. "We are **going for broke** now," Frankie says.

If you think that Frankie is threatening to injure you, go to **page 164**.

If you think that Frankie is talking about finishing the heist, go to **page 168**

[CHAPTER FOUR]

~Down to a Fine Art

"I THINK WE have to get out of here," you tell Eric. "We can't do this. Just the two of us? It's impossible." You **cross your arms** and look at Eric. You expect a big argument to **break out**, but Eric doesn't **put up much of a fight**.

"Fine, fine," he says, though he is clearly disappointed. "It looks like we're not **cut out for this**. But we had a **window**, you know. Don't you think we should take it? With the two of us together, the odds of—"

"I'm sorry," you say. "Our **window of opportunity** is getting out and finding help. Let's **cut out** now and leave."

You feel too tired to stand. You lean against a wall for a moment's rest. The **room begins to spin**, and Eric moves to your side just as you feel your **knees buckle**.

"I'm okay," you say, grabbing his arm. "Let's get out of here and call the cops."

You walk to one of the locked emergency exits, making sure that no one sees you. Eric tries each of the keys on the key ring, but none of them opens the door.

"Maybe our **best bet** is the main entrance."

A patrol of security guards walks past you as they **make their way** to the Main Hall. You and Eric **keep your heads down** and avoid **making eye contact** with any of them. You **hold your breath** and **cross your fingers**, and they pass right by you. They must believe you are part of the team.

At the main entrance, you see several guards posted at the doors. They are playing a card game. When you approach, one of the guards **stands up** and holds out his hands. "*Excusez-moi*, **not so fast**," he says.

"What's wrong? We're just going outside to **get some fresh air**," Eric says, trying to walk past them.

The guard doesn't budge. "You know Maddy's rules," he says, side-stepping in front of Eric to block his way. Eric gives the guard a rude look, but the man doesn't react. "**No one in, no one out.**"

"Come on," Eric pleads. He shows him the cigarette he received from Barrett. "I just want to smoke."

The guard **raises an eyebrow**. "Really? We are **down to the wire** at the main exhibit. We cannot risk opening the doors now. Especially not for smoke breaks."

Eric begins to **roll up** his sleeves, and you worry a **fight will break out**. The other guards now **stand up**, making the situation even more tense.

"**Calm down**, everyone," the first guard says. He **clears his throat** and pats Eric on the chest. "We do not even have the keys to open the doors. They took them all away."

"Who took your keys?" Eric asks.

"Your friends. Maddy's crew. We are just here to make sure no one gets in or out."

The two other guards, sensing a **change in the air**, return to **playing cards**.

"And what do I do about this?" Eric asks, shoving the cigarette in the guard's face. "See this? I've been waiting for this all day. Where am I supposed to enjoy my smoke?"

"If you need to smoke, do it here," the guard says.

He **makes a show** of **lighting up** a cigarette of his own and blows rings of smoke in Eric's face. The smell of smoke makes you want to gag, and you start to feel dizzy again. Around you, the men shift uneasily. You can tell Eric is about to **blow his top**. If a fight **breaks out**, you are both in deep trouble.

You decide to **take matters into your own hands**. With a loud groan, you collapse to the floor, making the fall as dramatic as possible. You clutch at your stomach.

"What's wrong?" Eric asks, kneeling down next to you.

You groan louder and with more emphasis.

"Look," Eric pleads with the guard. "We need to get him outside. He needs some fresh air."

The guard looks down at you. "What is wrong with him?"

"Hurry! He'll **pass out**, and you'll have a **mess on your hands**," Eric warns.

"*Ça alors*, I am sorry," the guard stammers. "Look, here is my key card. Go to the security station. No one is there right now. Go **hang out** with your friend, get some water, and have your smoke. Just do not **make a scene** here."

Eric grabs the key from the guard. You stumble to your feet and lean on Eric's arm. Slowly, you **make your way** out of the Main Hall and go back to the corridor to find the security station.

"Are you okay?" Eric asks. "I guess the front entrance is **crossed off our list**. Sorry about that."

"Well," you reply. "Do I win the Academy Award?" You smile knowingly.

"Idiot," Eric says, grinning back. "You **had me** back there."

"I had to get you away from that guard before things **took a turn for the worse**."

"I would have fought all three of them," Eric confesses.

"I know," you say. "That's why I had to **step in**. It could have turned into a brawl."

"At least now we have this," Eric says, waving the key card. "I never thought about **hiding out** in security."

You agree, but you also **point out** the guard's words. "What do we do? It sounds like they're almost finished. Final stages. **In no time**, they'll **take off** with the painting. We need to do something now." You pause. "And what about Darla?"

Darla's name **hangs in the air** like cigarette smoke.

Eric looks at you. "We need to **get it down to a fine art** first."

If you think that Eric means you need to perfect a plan first, go to **page 141**.

If you think that Eric means you need to go to the main exhibit and save the painting first, go to **page 160**.

"We don't think this is a game. We're being serious," you tell Barrett. "Honestly."

"What did you say?" he growls. Flecks of spit hit you in the face. "You're joking about a game? You think this is a **comedy routine**?"

You must have said something wrong—again. You are at a **loss for words**, and your **brain spins in circles** trying to think of a way to fix this situation.

"I hate that Maddy lets Willie keep hiring idiots," Barrett mutters. "When we're done with this, I'm going to make sure we **screen** future candidates."

With a swift punch to the stomach, Barrett **drops you** to the floor. Then he turns to Eric, now cowering in one corner. "Both of you move to the main exhibit," he growls. "We'll find a way to make you useful **for a change**."

Go to **page 126.**

You nod and clap your hands. "Let's do this," you tell Eric, hyping yourself up. "Let's go and save the painting then! Main exhibit, here we come."

You summon all your strength and courage and **burst out** to the corridor that leads to the gallery facing the main exhibit. Eric tries to **keep up** with you. It is weird that your roles are strangely reversed now; he is the cautious one, while you are being bold.

"Wait!" Eric calls out. "Don't you think we should get a plan in order first—get it **down to a fine art** before we go and **crash the party**?"

You ignore him up until you see a metal security gate blocking the entryway. You **stop in your tracks**. "Oh," you say, deflated. "We'll have to find another way in."

"Yeah, we have to **figure this out**," Eric says, joining you. "First, let's **scope out** the area."

Eric crouches down behind some potted plants and fixtures and checks to see if the **coast is clear**. He looks around and then waves for you to follow.

"They've got some heavy-duty tools in there," he says, pointing to the main exhibit room. "From the sound of it, they're cutting through metal."

You listen to the screeching of metal bars being sheared to pieces. "But I don't see the painting."

In the middle of the room, where the *Girl with a Pearl Earring* should be, you see only a metallic case. You realize that it is like a clamshell cover that completely **seals off** the painting from view. Around the larger exhibit area is another barrier, a gate of thick metal bars that extends from floor to ceiling.

"I read about this," you say. "It's a two-stage security barrier. You have to break through two layers of security to reach the painting. **State-of-the-art**."

"What are they doing?" Eric asks, indicating the crew.

"First, they'll have to cut the bars to get closer to the case."

"And then what? I doubt they'll want to cut the case open. They might accidentally damage the painting."

"They'll have to unlock it somehow and force the metal case to drop down."

Someone **creeps up** from behind you. "Well, look what I've found," a familiar voice says.

"What did you say?" Eric asks you.

"I didn't say anything," you tell Eric.

When you **turn around**, you see Barrett, Maddy's giant Australian henchman, smiling at you.

Eric jerks back, almost **knocking you over**. He signals for you to run, but you can't get your legs to move properly. You crash to the ground clumsily. The big man moves closer. He is so big that he **casts a shadow over you**.

"What are the two of you doing?" he demands. "This time, you better give me a good answer."

"At the moment," you say, "we're wondering why we even got out of bed this morning."

"Careful," he warns. "We don't want to **step on each other's toes**."

Go to **page 126**.

You decide to return and help Eric. He needs you right now. Alone in that room, he will be a **sitting duck**. If the thieves **break through** his barricade, there is **no telling** what they will do to him.

You **dash back** to the security room just in time to see three men taking positions around the windows. Two of them have **picked up** chairs and are slamming them against the bulletproof glass and door. Still safe inside, Eric taunts them by **making faces** and crude gestures. When he sees you standing there in the doorway, his face changes, and he accidentally **gives away** your location.

"Look! Another one!" a man says, pointing at you. He drops his chair and barrels toward you, pushing the other chairs and tables out of his way. He slams into your shoulder, forcing you back into the wall. You heave and **spit up** blood.

"Get that door open, yeah?" he calls out to the other men who **stand by**, watching.

While he gives them orders, you look around for a weapon and see a small fire extinguisher in the corner. You take it out of its holder and lie on top, hiding it from view.

"Not that way!" your attacker tells his men. "Keep hitting the door with the chair!"

You **stand up** slowly. The fire extinguisher feels cold in your hands, and you make sure you have a good grip on it. Just as the man turns back to deal with you, you bring the metal cylinder down on his head. He falls to the ground like a **bag of rocks**.

Alarmed that their boss is **down for the count**, the other men start to move away from the enclosure. Eric uses their panic **to his advantage**. He slides the hammer out of the door, comes out, and aims the tool at one of the men.

"Boom!" Eric shouts as the hammer **hits its mark**.

The third man tries to leave the room and clumsily smashes into a table.

"Get him!"

You rush over with the extinguisher held tightly in your hands.

The man looks at you with his hands up in the air. "Please don't!" he pleads.

You hesitate, but Eric runs over and punches the man in the face, **knocking him out**.

"You idiot!" Eric yells at you as he **catches his breath**.

"Well, you're welcome," you say, surprised and hurt at Eric's reaction. The adrenaline is starting to **wear off**. "I didn't want to leave you here to fight them alone."

"We didn't need to fight them at all," he says angrily. "All you've done is **waste time**. Darla's still **out there**, and there will be more thieves and guards coming here to **figure out** what happened when these guys don't **report in**. We'll have to change our plans now."

"I'm—I'm sorry," you **blurt out**. You hadn't thought about the consequences. You just wanted to help your friend.

"**Back to square one**!" Eric says.

If you think that Eric means you should go to the main exhibit, the central square-shaped room in the museum, go to **page 160**.

If you think that Eric means you should now follow the original plan, go to **page 165**.

Frankie is threatening to injure you. You glare at him defiantly. "You're not breaking me!" you roar back.

You **pick up** one of the tools and throw it at him. The wrench hits Frankie in the chest. The guards and thieves around you react with surprise. You wait for someone to attack you, but even Frankie seems confused.

"What the hell is wrong with you?" he bellows.

You realize your mistake. Frankie had no idea who you were. Until now. You have **given yourself away**.

"**Wait a minute**," he says. "I recognize you!"

You try to run.

"Grab him!" he orders the guards.

You fight back, but there are too many of them. Frankie **picks up** the wrench you threw and walks toward you. "Stupid kid," he says. "You've come to the **lion's den**."

Then he grabs you by the throat. You fight his grasp, but he is too strong. The room starts to spin. You gasp for air. Everything **goes black**.

Go to **page 182**.

You leave and go find Darla. Eric is right. Darla is in immediate danger, and she needs your help. Eric can **handle himself**. Plus, it might delay things. Keeping several of Maddy's crew busy dealing with a pesky tourist means they aren't working on cutting through to the *Girl with a Pearl Earring*. It might help delay the thieves' plan to steal the painting.

On your way to the second floor, you pass a cluster of exhibits. It is strange to see the gallery rooms completely empty now, with no one to admire the artwork inside. Just a few hours ago, this place was swarming with visitors **standing shoulder to shoulder**. As strange as it seems, you miss the noise and distraction of the crowds.

Up ahead, you see signs that point in the direction of the main exhibit. You go the opposite way. Your goal is to find Darla, though she could be anywhere by now. Looking around for other markers, you find one that points you to a familiar gallery.

Poterie et Vases

Have you been in the Pottery and Vases gallery before? Your memory of this part of the museum is **fuzzy** now, and you wish you didn't leave behind the rest of your belongings, including your map of the museum.

When you reach the entrance to the gallery, you see that the room is sealed shut behind a security gate. A security camera in one corner is turning side to side. You wave at it, hoping Eric can still access the monitors and work the console. Through the metal grill of the gate, you can see shards of a broken vase on the floor.

The gate **lifts up**, letting you inside. You **take a moment** to investigate the broken pieces, even holding up a jagged shard to the camera and letting Eric see possible evidence that Darla was around. You also hope that the **sight** of the broken vase will keep Eric **on his toes** as he watches the monitors.

"This must be the vase she was holding when we saw her earlier," you say into your walkie-talkie.

"I know," Eric says. "You better **hoof it**. She must be close by. Maybe you can still **catch up** with her."

You **spot** some damage in a display case up ahead. "Eric, open up that gate," you say, pointing in one direction. After a moment, the gate lifts. "Geez, this place is a maze," you remark, walking through.

The front of the display is broken, and shattered glass is scattered everywhere. You can tell a struggle **took place**. You imagine that someone was pushed hard against the display case. A smear of blood on the floor puts you on **high alert**.

"Someone's been hurt."

"Let's hope it's not Darla."

"Do you see her on any of the other cameras?" you ask. There is no response. "Eric? Eric, answer me!"

"Sorry, Sammy. I've **got company**," he says frantically. More of Maddy's men must have arrived at the security room. "Hurry through the galleries. Let me know which gates you want opened. I'll leave the channel open."

You hurry, running to and from each gallery, hoping to **run into** Darla or to find more clues of her being there. Are you on the **right track**? After several minutes, you hear the faint sound of power tools squealing nearby.

"I think I'm back near the main exhibit room," you say. "I've circled back around. There's no **sign** of Darla. I think I've **lost her trail**."

"There!" Eric yells. "I see her on the monitor. She's moving fast. It looks like—"

Eric stops and screams at someone in the security room.

"Step away from the monitors," you hear someone yell back.

The men must have broken through the door. Should you **double-back** and help your friend? You stand **frozen in place**, not sure what to do next.

All of a sudden, the sound on the walkie-talkie **cuts out**.

"Eric?" you say.

You tap the device. It crackles briefly and then goes silent. The battery is **dead**.

Go to **page 192**.

Frankie is talking about finishing the heist. You keep your back to Frankie and cheer along with the guards and thieves who are now working to get the *Girl with a Pearl Earring* out of its thick metal enclosure. After this, the thieves will switch to the final phase of their plan—their escape.

"**Final bend**, boys. Work as quickly as you can," Frankie orders. "It's **all or nothing** now. If you don't want to be here when the cops arrive, we better hurry!"

"He's a grumpy one," a guard whispers to you as Frankie walks away.

"Yes," you agree. "Let's get as far away from him as we can."

Following the group, you **make your way** to the main exhibit. Maddy is **walking in your direction**, barking orders to the other guards and crew members. You **take a quick glance** over your shoulder and lower your head as she walks past you.

"Go **sweep** the exit paths and make sure **everything is clear** for us," she orders someone. Then, to the crew working on the metal case, she says, "Whatever you do, don't damage the painting when it's being removed. I also want the canvas out of the frame. Do it gently, boys. This is our **payday**."

Maddy then **whirls around** and points at you. "And you," she says. "You're coming with me as soon as they open that case."

You **heart stops** for a moment, but you keep your composure. You quietly follow Maddy as she walks around the room and observes the various members of her crew packing bags and **clearing out** evidence. She writes notes on her clipboard at each stop. You marvel at how well she commands her gang of thieves and at the way everyone listens to her with absolute respect—maybe with fear. Even the goons twice her size **hang on every word** she says.

When her rounds are finished, she leads you back to the end of the room where the *Girl with a Pearl Earring* is hidden inside a thick metal case. The case surrounds the frame and canvas. **Up close**, it looks like a metal cube or block.

Maddy's men don't use cutting tools. Instead, they switch to large discs that they slide over the case. You hear muffled clicks from within the block's base. After several more clicks, the metal sheath around the painting begins to **slide down**. The discs seem to be controlling the metal cover, forcing it to drop.

The *Girl with a Pearl Earring* is revealed at last.

Maddy whoops with delight. After a short celebration, she snaps her fingers at one of the men. The man pulls out a knife and walks over to the frame.

"Remember," Maddy warns him, "pull it from the frame and detach the canvas carefully. If that knife does any damage to the painting, you'll **share the pain**."

"Of course, Maddy," the man answers, his knife poised in the air.

Like a surgeon about to perform a delicate operation, he begins slowly but methodically. He works the knife in gently at the seams of the frame and eases the canvas out. Everyone in the room watches him, hypnotized and **holding their breath**—even you.

In a **matter of minutes**, the painting is freed from its frame, and the man presents it to Maddy. She holds her arms out and takes the canvas like a sacred offering.

"We have it!" she announces, her voice booming in the exhibit room.

Loud cheers erupt. With a **delicate touch**, Maddy **rolls up** the canvas as gently as possible and puts it into a cylinder tube. She **runs** her long fingers down the leather casing of the container, caressing it.

Suddenly, she **makes eye contact** with you. "You, come with me," she instructs.

For a moment, you think that Maddy will recognize you, but she doesn't react when she looks you in the face. Strangely, you feel a sense of disappointment. But it is no wonder your face **doesn't a ring a bell**; it must be your scruffy appearance. You are tired, bruised, and **beat up**. If you looked in a mirror right now, you probably wouldn't even recognize yourself.

You have no other choice but to follow along. Just as you and Maddy start to walk away, a man runs into the exhibit room, screaming and waving his arms.

"The police! The police are here, Maddy!" the man yells.

The entire crew—thieves and security guards—start to panic. People scramble to gather their things.

"**Clear out** now. Leave nothing behind!" Maddy orders.

She grabs your arm and pulls you toward the next room and through another exhibit. You struggle to **keep up** with her as you zigzag through a maze of galleries and half-opened gates. At the next turn, she **stops short**. You find yourself staring at a closed gate.

Maddy seems confused. "This was supposed to be opened."

Before you can reply, she orders you to find another way out. You run through the maze of galleries until you find a route near the main exhibit that leads back to the construction area behind the museum.

You return to find Maddy now shedding her heavy black coat. "I think I found a way," you say. You give her the directions.

"Got it," she says, nodding. "Hold this." She **hands** you the leather tube. "And don't drop it."

You stare in awe. In the palm of your hands, you hold the *Girl with a Pearl Earring*. Estimated worth? Oh, just millions.

"We were supposed to have a clear path to the parking garage," Maddy mutters, removing her sweater. "Someone's **messed up big time**. I'll have to **come up** with another plan to get to my escape car."

You stare open-mouthed at Maddy, not sure what to do.

Maddy **stretches out** her hand to you. "Well, come on," she says impatiently. "**Hand it over**."

If you decide to give Maddy the painting, go to **page 171**.

If you decide *not* to give Maddy the painting, go to **page 172**.

You decide to give Maddy the painting. "Here you go, Maddy," you say, handing her the tube.

She slings the painting over her shoulder. You stare at her, hoping she will look at you again and **make the connection** this time, but her attention is focused on the pile of clothes at her feet.

"Be a dear and **clean up after me**. I will have to **travel light** if I'm going to get out of here." She kicks the pile in your direction and then turns around. "Leave the country and be sure to check your bank account," she adds, before darting away into the darkness.

You open your mouth to say something, but nothing **comes to mind**. You watch helplessly as Maddy disappears from sight, the priceless painting slung over her shoulder. Kicking at the pile of clothes on the floor, a tinge of sadness **comes over you**. You are oddly disappointed that she didn't recognize you.

Suddenly, your shoe hits a stiff object buried in the pile. You nudge it cautiously with your toe, and it clatters on the tiled floor. Searching through the clothes, you find Maddy's clipboard. Did she leave it for you to find?

On the front page is your name with a strange note by it.

AN ARM AND A LEG

Back at the main exhibit, the police have arrived. They **round up** a few of the rogue security guards working for Maddy. As they approach you, you **hold up** your hands in surrender. Once in custody, you tell them about the hostages in the East Wing. All you can do is hope they will believe your story.

Go to **page 178**.

You decide *not* to give Maddy the painting. "No, Maddy," you tell her. "If I'm going to give this to anyone, it won't be you." You grip the leather tube containing the painting in your hands.

"Give me the tube."

"No way."

"Be smart about this," Maddy says, watching you sling the tube over your shoulder. "The police are almost here.

"Good."

"Sammy, if I'm **going down**, I'm **taking you down** with me."

You pause and look at her in wonder. "So, you do recognize me."

Her eyes **flash** with anger. "Of course I do. And if I get caught, I'm going to tell them that you were a part of my crew and that you helped me steal the painting."

She grabs at the tube, but you **take a step** back, avoiding her. Her eyes narrow, but you can still see her green irises.

"Get back here now!" she orders.

You **take off running**. To your surprise, Maddy **gives chase**. You wonder why she decides to chase you rather than **make her escape**. Then it **dawns on you**: The painting is **her prize**. She **can't bear** to let it **slip from her grasp**.

You manage to squeeze your way under a partially open gate at the entrance to another gallery. Before Maddy reaches you, you pull down the metal barrier, blocking her. She **doesn't bother** trying to raise the gate. She simply stands there, calmly staring at you through the bars.

"Sammy," she says, "give me the painting. **Slip it through** the bars. I don't have much time."

You shake your head. "It's over, Maddy," you say. "I'm going to **hand this over** to the police. You might as well get out of here. It won't be too late for you if you go now."

"I can't do that," she insists. She then rattles the gate furiously. "You don't **get it**! If I leave here without that painting, certain people will **hunt me down**."

*Hunt her down? Does she mean buyers are expecting to have the painting delivered to them? This woman has **some nerve**.*

You can hear people shouting in French coming in your direction. You look at Maddy, but she doesn't **budge from her spot**.

"Sammy, please," Maddy begs. "I'll **make it worth your while**. How much do you want?"

"Nothing. This painting doesn't belong to me or you."

With the police coming closer, Maddy realizes your mind is **made up**. "Fine, then. How do I get out of here?"

All of a sudden, you have a **change of heart** about letting her escape. Why should Maddy **get away with this**, especially after what she and her men **put you** and your friends **through**?

"I've had **second thoughts**. I—I can't help you," you tell her blankly.

Before she can say anything, you turn away and walk toward the voices. You take the tube and **hold it up** in the air and raise your other hand. As soon as the police **come in**, you plan to surrender and tell them everything.

But something is wrong. The police aren't running in your direction. A swarm of officers stand on the opposite side of the gate—where Maddy is. They look from her to you, not sure what to do.

"Over here! I'm over here!" you yell as loudly as you can. But it is **no use**.

"Help! *Aidez moi!*" Maddy shouts, pointing at you. "That thief is taking the *Girl with a Pearl Earring!*"

Before you can protest, Maddy **takes out** her wallet and shows them her fake museum credentials.

"I've been taken hostage," she explains. Then she nods in your direction. "*Il est celui que vous voulez.* He's the one you want."

Pretending to be a museum worker seems to have worked. The police have **put their sights on you** now. You panic as the police try to get the gate open. They have lost interest in Maddy and now want to **take you in**.

*How many **backup plans** does Maddy have?*

You **turn around** and run. You decide to **head back** out to the construction site. Realizing that you are still wearing the museum uniform, you **ditch** the jacket by a pile of bricks. With a **heavy heart**, you **take a long look** at the art tube. For a moment, you think about leaving it there for someone else to find.

It's not my problem . . . Then you stop yourself. *No, I can't risk it **falling back** into Maddy's hands.*

Slinging the art tube off your shoulder, you take the rolled canvas out of its container and stuff it inside your shirt. You find a window and drop down to a walkway. In no time, you are on the street. In front of the museum, a large group of onlookers has gathered to watch the police **take up** positions at the entrance. Silently, you **slip into the crowd** unnoticed and watch the suspects being taken outside in handcuffs.

Most of the people being taken into custody are the local French security guards, but one of the detainees is a man from Maddy's crew who struggles and protests in English. As he is being **dragged out**, you notice that he is pointing at something or someone.

"I knew it!" he keeps saying. "I knew she was Interpol!"

You **follow his gaze** and see a woman standing off to the side covered in a blanket. When she **looks up**, you see her face and nearly faint. It is Darla.

You run toward her. "Darla!" you call out. Several policemen try to stop you, but you dodge them. "Darla!"

"Sammy!" she says, seeing you. You embrace. Bruised and tired, Darla **looks worse for the wear**, but she is happy to see you.

"What's going on?" you ask.

"A lot," Darla says, wincing in pain. "There was an art heist today, but we stopped it."

"We?" you ask, **playing dumb**.

She smiles. "I'm with Interpol. I've been investigating these crooks for a while now, and I followed them here. I'm sorry I didn't tell you sooner, but I didn't know for sure if I could trust you and Eric."

"Where is Eric?"

"Somewhere around here. He was found in a suit of armor **fighting off** some of the criminals. The police are going to question him, but I'm sure they'll let him go." Darla takes your hand and holds it tightly. "I'm glad you're safe," she says.

You decide not to tell her about your day just yet. You look over at the criminals being hauled out of the museum. When the last police officer exits, you wonder what happened to Maddy.

"Is that all of them?"

"Enough of them," Darla says, though she seems disappointed.

"What's wrong?" you ask.

"Nothing," she says, walking away.

You look over Darla's shoulder. The screaming man has pressed his face against the police car's window.

Another car comes to **pick you up**. Darla rides with you to the police station where you wait for Eric to be released after some routine questioning. The police also ask you a few questions. All through the briefing, you say nothing about the canvas rolled up tight inside your shirt. Eventually, they let you go.

While you and Eric are happy to see each other, you notice that Darla and the rest of the authorities are disappointed that the painting is gone.

"Let's go out to dinner," you suggest to Darla, hoping to surprise her with your secret and **cheer her up**.

"I can't," she says. "I have to interrogate these security guards. Can you believe they would **sell out** their friends for money?"

"Loyalty is hard to find these days," Eric says, putting his arm around you.

You smile. "You'll find the painting," you tell Darla. "I'm sure of it."

"Thanks, Sammy," Darla says, tears **welling up** in her eyes. "I really hope you're right. It would be a great loss if we didn't."

Back at the hostel, you and Eric pack your belongings for the **next leg** of your trip.

"The stories we'll tell!" Eric repeats, rambling on about the events at the museum. "I can't wait to tell people **back home** what happened to us."

You relive the moments with him until you both fall asleep.

In the **middle of the night**, you **wake up** and take the rolled canvas out to the common area. The room is empty and quiet. You find a table near a window and unroll the *Girl with a Pearl Earring* for one last look. As you study the etched lines and deep colors under the moonlight, you realize how beautiful the painting actually is. You never appreciated it before. You look at the young girl in the portrait. Her gaze is honest and intimate. She looks as if she is about to share a secret with her viewers—with you. It is truly astonishing. As you stare at the girl with the mysterious gaze, you wonder about what she is thinking and what she knows.

"This will be our little secret," you whisper to yourself.

You have no intention of keeping the painting of course. For the rest of the night, you think of a way to return it to the authorities.

THE NEXT MORNING, Eric **wakes up**, excited and refreshed.

"Can you believe it? I finally **slept like a log**," he tells you. "I think **catching the bad guys** suits me."

"I didn't sleep much," you say, yawning.

"Oh? Why not?"

"Some **unfinished business**," you say, grinning.

As you both **check out** of the hostel, you **drop off** a note in the hostel's mailbox with Darla's phone number and the link to the Interpol website. Once you and Eric have left Lyon, you plan to send Darla an e-mail telling her to expect a call from the hostel. You wish you could be there to see her face when she discovers what you have done.

While Eric **makes small talk** with some of the other hostel guests, you **take one last look** at a framed painting on the wall in the hallway. A group of tourists have stopped to appreciate what they think is an amazing replica of the *Girl with a Pearl Earring*.

"It looks so real!" one woman remarks.

"Did you hear about the robbery?" her companion asks. "The real painting's been stolen. The authorities are frantic, and the museum is closed for the rest of the summer."

"How horrible," the woman says, shaking her head, but her **eyes are fixed** on the painting on the wall.

You smile, watching them as they experience the famous painting **up close and personal**. You have to stifle the urge to **blurt out** your secret.

If only they knew . . .

You trust that the canvas will be safe behind the glass **for the time being**. Before you leave, you **take a picture** of the hallway wall with Eric's phone.

"**Last minute** souvenir?" Eric asks as he stands by your side.

"The *Girl with a Pearl Earring*," you tell him, pointing at the wall. "She's a beauty, isn't she?"

"We saw the **real thing** yesterday," he scoffs. "I've got tons of pictures, thanks to Darla."

"Lucky you."

You almost tell him what you did last night but decide to save the story for a special occasion.

THE END

One by one, the police take the suspects outside in handcuffs. You cooperate with the investigators, giving them as much information as possible, but they remain suspicious of you. They keep you in handcuffs and **trot you out** with the other criminals. The bright light of day burns your eyes, and you squint when you look out at the gathering of people standing outside.

"Sammy?" someone calls out to you.

You turn to see Darla standing near one of the police cars. She looks bruised and weary but smiles at you with a toothy grin.

"Darla!" you say with joy. "You're safe!"

Darla rushes over and demands you be let go. She argues with a police officer in French and **takes out** a badge. Immediately, the cop **spins you around** and takes the handcuffs off your wrists.

"I guess you're the Interpol agent," you say with genuine awe. "Nice."

"How did you know?"

"**A little bird told me**," you reply, smiling.

Darla sighs and **takes one long look** at you. "I'm sorry I kept it a secret from you this whole time."

"Why didn't you just tell us?"

"It was all part of my **cover**," she says apologetically. "I needed to make it believable that I was just a tourist traveling through Europe. Maddy and her crew have **eyes and ears everywhere. For what it's worth**, you and Eric **made it a breeze** for me."

"Where is Eric?" you ask.

"Interpol!" a voice interrupts.

Several policemen drag out one of Maddy's men. Even in handcuffs, the man manages to **twist around** and scream at Darla. Other officers rush over to subdue him, but he slips through and **runs in circles**, kicking and screaming.

"I knew it! She's Interpol!"

"Well, he seems angry," you comment. "Looks like you made friends."

"That's Willie for you. And yeah, we did get acquainted," Darla says with sarcasm. She turns to the police officers and waves her hand. "Get him out of here."

"I'll get you!" Willie screams as the cops force him into a car. "One day, I'll get you all!" he keeps saying, even as the car speeds away.

You breathe a **big sigh of relief**.

At the police station, the police question you for hours. Darla visits you several times, giving you advice. When they finally let you go, Darla reunites you with Eric who has never been happier to see you.

When you return to the hostel, the desk clerk signals you over and gives you a note. You look at it briefly and then stuff it in your pocket for later. Now is the time to celebrate with your friends. The three of you go out for dinner.

"We've got a lot of stories to tell each other and everyone back home," he says, **elbowing you in the ribs**.

"I'll go first," you tell him.

You all share your versions of the events: the fire alarms, the power going out, your journey through the museum, and the scary run-ins with Maddy's crew.

When dinner ends, Darla tells you she must stay behind in France and continue the investigation. "Maddy is still out there," she says.

You remember the note stuffed in your pocket but decide to open it later.

"What's wrong?" Eric asks you later that night.

"Nothing. I'm just tired," you say, as you **fall face first** onto the bed.

Truthfully, you feel a wave of emotions as you try to process everything that has happened today. You met one of the world's most notorious art thieves and **lived to tell the tale**.

After Eric falls asleep, you **pull out** the note. On one side, it says:

AN ARM AND A LEG

Looking for more writing, you **turn over** the note and find various lines and boxes to be filled in like a form. You realize that the piece of paper is a bank deposit slip of some kind. It is for no bank you recognize, but you **have a hunch** about the mysterious message on the other side.

Down in the lobby, you log onto the hostel computer and visit your bank's website. You know it isn't the safest thing to do, but you need to **test your hunch**.

You put in your account username and password. An alert **pops up**, telling you that a message has been left for you in your inbox. You click the message and read it.

Dear Sammy,

You said you would help me steal the painting, and you **came through**. Thank you. I suppose you told the cops most of what happened today. Still, I'm thankful for all your help. Here's something for your trip around Europe. It won't buy you an island, but at least you can keep your arm and leg.

- MdC

Hands shaking, you review your account balance and look at the most recent deposit. You almost **pass out** when you see the amount.

THE NEXT MORNING at **checkout**, the front desk clerk tells you that a package has been delivered for you.

You shrug. "I'm not expecting anything," you say, though you know it has to be connected to the earlier note you got.

"What is it?" Eric asks.

You unwrap an art tube.

"Is it from Darla?" Eric wonders.

You pop open the tube and **roll out** a poster-size print of the *Girl with a Pearl Earring*. Eric takes the poster and begins to comment on it, but you **pay no attention** as you continue to check the package.

Reaching in, you **pull out** a glossy brochure and another note. The brochure is for another museum in France with an announcement for a special exhibit to come. A Picasso collection that includes *The Old Guitarist* will be **on view** in a few months.

You read the note. Your heart **skips a beat** when you see the words in Maddy's handwriting.

SEE YOU THERE?

THE END

You **wake up** in a daze. Your head hurts, and your eyes go **in and out of focus**.

Frankie is standing over you. You can hear him **cracking his knuckles**. "I'm going to **teach you a lesson**," he says. "A permanent one." He reaches down and slaps the back of your head. You almost **black out** again. "Why are you here?" Frankie questions. "Tell me who you are." Frankie punches you in the face. "Answer me!"

Everything **goes sideways** when Frankie kicks your chair over, knocking you to the ground. The impact sends a **shockwave through your body**, and you scream in pain. You can feel blood dripping from your nose and mouth.

"Sammy!" you hear.

"How—how do you know my name?" you ask in a delirious state. "What do you want from me?"

"Sammy!" you hear again.

"What do you want?"

You question your eyes when you see two Frankies standing before you. You close them tight and look again. The two Frankies begin punching each other.

"What's going on?" you blabber. "Why—why are you hitting yourself?"

"Sammy!" one of the Frankies yells at you again.

You hear a clanking sound, metal rubbing against metal. Staring hard at Frankie, you slowly regain your focus. You blink fast, and the blurry scene sharpens before your eyes: Frankie is fighting with a knight in a full suit of armor.

"Surrender!" the knight demands, holding a sword against Frankie's throat.

Am I having a crazy dream?

Frankie **holds up** his hands and backs away until he reaches the wall.

"Don't move, knave!" the knight commands. "Or I'll **run you through** with Excalibur." The knight looks back toward you and orders you to **get up**. "Sammy, I need you to get out of that chair," he says.

Your hands are tied behind your back around the chair's frame, but you manage to separate yourself from the seat.

"Good. Loop your arms under your legs if you can," the knight instructs.

You struggle to loosen yourself from the ropes. The knight tells you to **roll over** to him. It takes several moments before he cuts you free with his sword.

"Now, **stand up** and grab that rope. **Tie up** the guy for me."

When **all is said and done**, the knight grabs you by the shoulders and shakes you forcefully. "Sammy!" he says. He **lifts up** his headpiece, and you recognize your friend.

"Eric?"

"Yeah, it's me."

"What's with the medieval **get-up**?"

Eric laughs. "Yeah, you're going to be all right."

Behind him, you can see the police **storming the room**. Then you **black out** again.

Go to **page 178**.

You decide to go downstairs to look for Eric. You wonder whether it is possible the two of you can **make it out** of this museum safely.

At first, you feel utterly alone; there isn't a living, breathing soul **in sight**. This morning, you couldn't wait to get out of here. Now, with everything that has happened, you find yourself wishing for a museum filled with visitors.

"Eric!" you whisper into the walkie-talkie.

Nothing.

"Eric, it's Sammy," you say, knowing it is risky to use your name. "If you're there, change the frequency on your walkie-talkie to your favorite number and change the channel to mine."

You wait in silence for what feels like days until you hear a familiar voice. "Hello?"

"Eric! You're there!"

"Totally, Sammy!" he responds cheerfully. "Great idea, by the way, on the numbers. We'll have some privacy for a while. We should keep switching frequencies and channels to keep them **off our back**."

"We should also **keep it short**. Where are you?"

"I think I just found the security room. I see a console here with a ton of buttons and switches. There are also a few displays, but none of them are really working. What about you?"

You look around for a sign.

Arts Modernes

"The Modern Arts gallery, I think," you say.

None of the pieces in the room look like anything recognizable, but you don't have the time to critique any of it.

"What would that be in French?" Eric mumbles to himself. "Oh, that one's easy. *Arts Modernes*. Okay, I see some scribbling here."

A security gate starts to fall at the entrance. Gears whine and squeak as it is lowered to the floor.

"The gate is coming down," you say.

"Okay. Tell me what happens now."

"They're lifting off the ground."

"Oh, and look here. *Camera de securite*. I think I'm **getting the hang of this**." Eric chuckles. "I guess I know more French than I thought. **Turn around**."

High up in the corner of the room, a camera swivels in your direction. You wave at it.

"I see you," Eric sings.

"What do you see on the other monitors?"

"More gallery rooms. The picture quality isn't all that great on these monitors. I just see a bunch of rooms with stuff."

"Anything familiar? Anything near the main exhibit or the museum entrance?"

"Nope. Why? You got some sort of plan?"

"I can't find Darla. I can go to you and—"

"I've got another idea," Eric interrupts. "You **up for** being a hero?"

"What are you talking about?"

"Since I'm in control here, I figure we could **mess around** with the thieves a little bit."

"I don't know if that's a good idea," you say. You don't want to **rile them up** anymore than you already have. "We should probably work on getting out of here and notifying the police."

"Going to have to disagree with you there, buddy," he says. "No one steals a painting when Eric is **in the house**."

"Eric, it's hardly the right time. If anything, we need to find Darla."

"I'm checking the cameras now," Eric says, his voice **trailing off**. "Oh, look here! She looks familiar."

"Who?"

"Not sure. It's all in black and white and far away."

"Where is it? I can go **scope it out**," you say.

"Hard to say. I see paintings and sculptures."

"That's like everywhere else," you hiss. "What else?"

"Well, I can see the main exhibit in the background."

"Okay. I'll **head** there now."

"Be careful!"

The walk to the main exhibit gallery is slow and dangerous. Besides almost running into a security guard on patrol, you nearly **knock over** a display in the dark. In one of the rooms filled with sculptures, you narrowly avoid getting gored by a statue of a tree.

"I'm almost there," you tell Eric, **spotting** the area where you lost your friends as you daydreamed in line earlier. You **come across** the painting of the street vendor and have **mixed feelings**. "I know where I am," you tell Eric. "I can see the main exhibit from here."

"**Keep a low profile**," Eric tells you.

"They can't see me. I can barely see them as it is."

"**Check this out**," Eric says.

Lights begin to flicker overhead, and the security gate for the main exhibit drops down. The thieves shout in surprise.

"What are you doing?"

"Exactly what I planned," Eric says. "Now, let me know what happens next."

More shouting comes from the back of the room. Inside the main exhibit, the thieves begin to scream at each other. The scene is total chaos.

"What's going on over there?"

"They were starting to cut through the barrier around the *Girl with a Pearl Earring*. The alarms earlier must have triggered a lockdown. The painting itself is covered and protected by a metal case. But it looks like the thieves have the right tools. They'll get through soon enough."

"What do we do?"

"We should get out of here and call the police," you say, trying to control your irritation. Eric is enjoying this too much. He is **clueless** about the possible dangers.

"You're no fun, Sammy."

"With all the commotion you caused, I'm guessing they'll be sending someone your way to **figure out** who's been **messing with** the security gates. You need to **abandon ship**."

"How about I meet you there?" Eric asks. "I'll leave now."

"Okay, but don't get lost," you tell Eric. "And no crazy stunts."

Go to **page 188.**

You wait for Eric and hope he doesn't **run into trouble** on his way over to you.

"You hear me?" Eric says, breathing heavily.

"I do. What's wrong?" you ask, sensing something is wrong.

"Um, I'm sort of stuck. Can you come and get me?"

"Where are you?"

"I'm out of the office section. You really need to get over here fast," Eric says.

"Where?" you ask impatiently.

"Medieval something," Eric says.

You **pull out** the map in your pocket and look for the section Eric is talking about. "Okay. I'm **on my way!**"

The way over to the gallery is uneventful. In minutes, you are standing at the entrance.

Outils Médiévales et Armory

"Eric," you whisper, looking around the exhibit. Glass displays of period costumes, weaponry, and other artifacts fill the room.

"Huzzah!" someone says, jumping behind you.

You **turn around** and **throw a punch**, but it misses completely.

"**Watch out!**" Eric says.

"What are you doing?" you ask, annoyed. "I thought you were in trouble." You stare in shock at his clothes.

"I wanted you to come over and help me **put on** this cool armor."

Eric is dressed in a security guard uniform, but a medieval tabard hangs over his shirt. He grips a metal helmet in his hands.

"You know you look ridiculous, right?"

"Here," Eric says, picking up and throwing a duffel bag at you. "There's another guard uniform inside. **Put it on.**"

You do as he says while he brandishes a sword. "Cool weapon, huh?" he says, thrusting it at an invisible opponent.

"We aren't here to fight, remember?" you tell Eric. "We need to get out of here."

"I'm here to be the museum's **knight in shining armor**," Eric says, handing you a chest piece. "Tie that on me, please."

"I'm not helping you **put on** more armor!"

"Did you hear that?"

"What are you talking—?"

Eric holds up a gloved fist, signaling for you to be quiet. He cranes his neck, and his eyes widen. "Behind you!" he yells as two guards enter the room.

"What are you two doing?" the guards ask.

Eric readies his sword, but you hold him back. "We're just **messing around**," you reply, laughing nervously.

"*Imbéciles*," one guard says, taking the armored chest piece away from you.

The guards talk in French and laugh hysterically at Eric. Their reaction is starting to piss off Eric. You watch nervously as he puts the helmet on and flips down the helm, covering his face.

"Eric, don't," you warn.

"What are you laughing at?" Eric accuses the guards.

"You, of course," a guard responds. The one holding the chest piece **walks up** to Eric and asks, "Can I be your loyal squire?"

Both of the guards start laughing again, and you can tell by Eric's posture that he isn't pleased.

"That's it," Eric says under his breath.

Before you can stop him, Eric hits the guard with the handle of his sword. The guard flies backwards and lands on his back, unconscious. When the other guard **pulls out** his walkie-talkie, Eric stabs at it with the sharp end, swiftly **knocking it out** of his hand. The guard **falls to his knees** as Eric points the blade at the man's face.

"Do you yield?" Eric asks, touching the tip of the sword to the man's chin.

"*Oui! Je me rends!*" the guard says.

"Good." With a sharp blow, Eric hits the man with the handle of his sword. The man falls to the ground, unconscious.

You run over to Eric who looks like he is in shock. "You okay?" you ask. You speak gently. "Why don't you give me the sword." You **hold out** your hand.

"I don't know what **got into me**," Eric says, looking around in a daze. He removes his helmet. The **blood rushes out** of his face. "That was crazy. I thought I was a real knight."

You point at the downed guards. "This is a problem," you say. "What do we do?"

"Hey! What the hell is happening here?" a gruff voice asks.

A large man dressed in black enters the room and looks around. His eyes widen when he **takes in** the two injured guards, a knight in full armor, and you.

"Barrett!" one of the guards says, waking up. "These two are trying to—"

"Quiet!" Barrett bellows.

By your side, Eric is fumbling with his armor. You start to apologize to Barrett when Eric **puts on** the helmet and charges the man. Without **breaking a sweat**, Barrett holds out his clenched fist and punches Eric **straight in the face**. The helmet is knocked loose, and your friend tumbles to the ground. Eric lies in a heap on the floor, groaning in pain.

You stare at Eric and then at Barrett in awe. "I assume Maddy probably didn't hire you for your delicate touch," you quip.

"You want yours, too?" Barrett asks, pointing at you with a beefy finger.

Immediately, you **hold up** your hands. "Uh, nope. **I'm good**."

"Get your friend. You're coming with me."

Go to **page 126**.

Tobin is only thinking about the loot they will be stealing, and it is better not to trust him. As much as Tobin looks like he wants to help you, he really is only **looking out for himself**. These are thieves, not charity workers, after all. Once he sees you are of no more use to him, he will probably **dump you** and **give you up** to Frankie or Maddy.

You think about your friends, Eric and Darla. Those are the people you care about. You **throw caution to the wind**.

"Tobin, I'm sorry," you **blurt out**. "Do what you need to do, but I can't do this. I'm not a thief, and I can't help you with the loot and **deliver the goods**. It would be wrong."

"That's not exactly what I meant—"

You apologize again and run for the exit. Scratching his head, Tobin stares back at you in shock.

You retrace your steps and carefully **make your way** back inside the museum's darkened main floor. You can hear the distant *whirring* of power tools as the thieves work on the painting in the main exhibit. You decide to stay as far away from them as possible and check the other parts of the museum.

Go to **page 192.**

Walking up to the second floor, you feel your exhaustion **taking its toll**. You are in **bad shape**. Your feet feel as heavy as stones. It seems like a **lifetime has passed** since you were asleep in bed this morning. But you **push aside any thoughts** of **giving up**. Your thoughts return to your friends, Darla and Eric. They need your help.

With nothing **out of the ordinary** on the second floor aside from the eerie quietness, you follow a hallway that leads to an intersection. Directional signs point to the left and to the right.

Galeries Principales
Des Expositions Spéciales

Another sign, a smaller one, indicates another destination down the hallway.

Toilettes

Go to **page 207**.

You feel anxious as you move from hiding spot to hiding spot. Security gates have **locked down** most of the galleries, but it also looks like several of the gates haven't been triggered or were stopped midway to the floor.

You wonder where Eric is. It is possible he just left when the museum was evacuated. He might be waiting at the entrance right now, wondering where you and Darla are. Too bad you don't have a cellphone to **reach out** to him. As for Darla, you don't want to imagine what might have happened to her. You know you have to find her.

Where would they have taken her?

Up ahead, you see a small sign.

Toilettes

It **couldn't hurt** to check.

Go to **page 207**.

To your surprise, the falling artifacts easily **knock out** the man. For now, you are safe. The next room, however, is packed with more art thieves. There is **no point** trying to **fight them off**. They won't **go down without a fight**. You will have to find a way out of this gallery section without **drawing their attention**.

You walk through empty gallery rooms, feeling terrified as well as excited. In any other circumstance, you would be tempted to explore the rooms just for the chance to see the paintings and other exhibits without the hassle of protective guards and annoying tourists. You **steal admiring glances** at a few pieces of art on the wall but continue on without stopping.

The museum is now very much a maze. You walk into one gallery only to find that security gates **close off** the other entrances to the space. You **backtrack, taking note** to avoid this area, and **head back** through another gallery. You move in and out of the various galleries, trying your best to remember the locations of the dead-ends. **In a pinch**, if the crew ever starts chasing after you, you would want to avoid these rooms. Using **trial and error**, you **do your best** to navigate the museum floor, **working your way** away from the Main Hall and far from the main exhibit.

Eventually, you enter a gallery with a view of the museum's main corridor. Unfortunately, a security gate blocks the gallery's other entrance. In the hallway, you look in both directions and consider your options. Somewhere nearby, you hear hushed voices and chatter. You aren't sure where it is coming from. Wanting to avoid **running into anyone**, you step back, look to your left, and walk down the corridor to go through another gallery.

You continue moving eastward until you finally find a gallery that has a possible opening back to the main exhibit. The room you enter is a large rotunda filled with Roman sculptures and busts.

Sculptures et Bustes Romains

Someone sneezes near you. You **turn around** to see a familiar face hiding near a set of busts.

"Darla!" you exclaim.

A **wave of relief washes over you**. She looks as astonished as you are and **leaps up** to greet you.

"*Qui est ce?*" says a security guard.

Your heart drops as two guards holding long sticks **move from the shadows**. In Darla's defense, you rush at one of the guards.

"Stop!" Darla shouts at you.

Just as you charge him, the guard steps to the side and grabs your right arm, **pinning it** behind your back. You scream in pain and **fall to your knees**.

"*Estes-vous fou?*" The guard lets you go, and you hold your burning shoulder.

"No, he's not crazy," Darla says, **bending down** to help you up. "He's **with me**. He's **one of us**."

You scan the guards' faces. They regard you suspiciously.

"I thought they were **holding you prisoner**," you tell Darla.

"No, they're here to help me. I found them upstairs, **tied up** in the bathrooms."

"Help you?" you say, confused.

Darla **takes a moment** to explain her mission.

"Oh, wow," you say. "I had no idea."

You are genuinely shocked to learn that your sweet friend is actually a **tough-as-nails**, undercover Interpol agent. Your **head spins**.

"It's insane, Darla. Does—does Eric know?"

Darla shakes her head. "For now, only you and my new allies here are **in on it**." Darla introduces the guards to you. "This is Georges and Emily."

The two guards nod at you. They look like **they have seen better days**. The weapons they hold in their hands are nothing more than the broken halves of broomsticks.

"*C'est* Sammy," Darla says, pointing at you.

Now that you have been reunited with Darla, your **thoughts turn** to your other friend being held captive. "Eric is with the thieves at the main exhibit," you explain.

"Then, that's where we're going," Darla says.

"Your other friend is *with* the thieves?" Emily asks.

"No, no. He's not **working with them**, but they have him," you clarify. "We were both captured, but I was able to escape."

"Let's hurry, then," Darla orders, **handing** you a long staff. "I found some weapons in one of the galleries. We can't **waste any more time**."

Together, you approach the main exhibit with a **sense of purpose**. You can see the crew is almost finished lowering the metal casing around the painting. Metal chunks of the protective cover are scattered on the floor. You can already see the top part of the *Girl with a Pearl Earring*. A pale forehead peeks through the casing. Off to the side, Eric is being **pushed around** by one of the rogue guards.

"I can see her!" Emily whispers, referring to the painting. "They're going to steal her if we don't stop them. We need to do something now."

You can tell that Darla wants to **work out** a plan first, but without a **second thought**, Emily runs into the room, her weapon raised high in the air.

"Wait!" Darla calls after her.

It is too late. Georges also **springs into action**, running into the fray. You hope that Emily and Georges are trained in hand-to-hand combat because with the crew's numbers the **odds are against you**.

As the fighting starts, you decide there is nothing else to do but **jump in, guns blazing**. You **grit your teeth** and race across the room, swinging your weapon in front of you to **keep at bay** the art thieves. Eric sees you and uses the distraction of your **sneak attack** to hit his captor from behind. The man falls on a pile of metal tools, hits his head, and gets **knocked out cold**.

"The painting!" Emily screams.

Before you can react, a man **charges you** and rams into your chest. The impact sends you stumbling backwards and onto the floor. Eric steps in front of you, **fending off blows** from your attacker. You get **back on your feet** and stand next to Eric as you **take turns** swinging at the man.

The room is in chaos. But **going for the first strike** has allowed you and your friends a chance to **level the playing field** by **knocking down** a few of the thieves **right off the bat**. You hear a snap as Georges's wooden stick **breaks against** a thief's back. The man recoils and falls to the ground. Several of the criminals have **picked up** their own weapons, and they start to **drive back** Darla and Emily.

Not all of Maddy's men are **fighting you off**. Two men are stationed at the painting, **working overtime** to bring down the metallic case covering it. Their tools emit heavy mechanical clicks. Metal scrapes against metal.

You watch in horror as the *Girl with a Pearl Earring* is eventually exposed. It is now **free for the taking**.

"Sammy, help!"

Eric is struggling with one of thieves and trying to get him in a headlock. You run toward them, your staff in hand. You slice through the air and hit the man on the back of the legs. He grunts in pain and crumples to the floor. Eric hits him again. The thief finally goes **out like a light**.

Emily screams. She **sets her eyes on** Maddy and runs to her. But before she can even get close, Barrett **steps in her way**. He lets Emily hit him **square in the chest** with her stick; it splinters on impact.

Barrett laughs. "Is that all you got, little lady?" he says mockingly. Before Emily can react, he shoves her aside, and she **falls down** and hits her head.

"Eric!" you yell, directing his attention to Barrett.

"Maddy's **taking off** with the painting," he yells back. "Go after her! I'll keep this one busy."

Eric leaps onto Barrett's back, and the two go spinning around the room. With Barrett busy dealing with Eric, the way to Maddy is now clear. You race toward her as she hurriedly puts the **rolled up** canvas into an art tube. After she **shouts out** an order to her men, she slings the tube on her shoulder. With a dramatic pause, she **looks you in the eye** and **holds your gaze** for a brief moment. She then winks and **takes off** running.

Suddenly, from **out of nowhere**, Darla lunges and tackles Maddy to the floor. They both tumble on the ground. Darla swings her wooden weapon at Maddy's knee but misses, hitting the marble surface instead. The stick breaks in half, and Maddy **pushes her off**. Darla makes another lunge for Maddy, but a guard **sneaks up** on her. He clasps her around the waist and **holds her back**.

Darla yells at her attacker, but the man **holds on** to her.

You **change course** to go to Darla's aid, but she screams at you and points at Maddy. "I can deal with this. Go after Maddy!"

All around the room, your friends are **fending off** attackers and **risking life and limb**. Meanwhile, Maddy is **running off** with the painting, **heading** deeper into the maze of galleries. If you blink, you might **lose sight of her**.

"The painting!" Darla cries, **breaking your concentration**.

You nod. You know what you need to do. You go after Maddy.

"Sammy!" Darla's voice echoes in the large room. "She'll probably go to the Main Hall. **Cut her off** before she escapes!"

> If you think that Darla is telling you to chase after Maddy through the maze of galleries and stop her *before* she reaches the Main Hall, go to **page 206**.

> If you think that Darla is telling you to stop Maddy's escape at the Main Hall, go to **page 212**.

"Let's go find some of the others," Darla suggests.

You and Darla **split up** from Jean and Georges and walk toward the galleries. Security gates block many of the entrances.

"These were moving earlier," Darla says. "But I guess they've stopped now. Look over there!"

In the corner, a rolled-up tapestry leans against the wall. A pair of black boots juts out from the bottom. Darla rushes over and begins to unroll the banner. Wrapped inside is a frightened guard **scared out of her wits**.

"*Laissez-moi partir!*" she yells after you pull the tape from her mouth.

"You're safe," you tell her.

She stares at you in shock as you untie her from her bindings. "Who are you?" she asks.

"Interpol," Darla says matter-of-factly, showing the woman her identification. "Do you speak English?"

"Yes. But it is **so-so**."

"It sounds excellent."

"Can you walk?" you ask.

"It is my head that hurts, not my feet."

"We found more guards **tied up** in the bathrooms," you tell her.

The woman's face brightens. "Where are they? Take me. Have you alerted the police?"

"Not yet," Darla says. "We've joined with some of your colleagues and **split up** into smaller search teams to look for the others who've been taken."

"It is awful," the guard says, **breaking down into tears**. "We were **taken prisoner** by our own friends. The alarms go off, and some guards begin to hit us. We were taken away and hidden."

"I'm so sorry," Darla says.

"This one friend . . . he told me he would keep me safe. Told me not to make a sound when he tied me up. He said he had to do it to make money for his family." The overwhelmed guard begins to sob and covers her face. "These thieves are smart and determined." She looks up at you. "**They will stop at nothing**. We must do something, oui? Please, *vous devez aider*. Help us!"

Darla embraces her. "We'll help."

"Emily!" Jean and Georges shout in unison when they see the guard you rescued.

The three colleagues look happy to see each other. They huddle into a group and embrace each other. Darla **gives them a moment** before she interrupts. They speak to each other in French for a while, and then the conversation becomes loud and angry until Darla orders them to stop.

"We need a plan," you say. "We can't **wait here in the wings** forever."

"Let's not **get ahead of ourselves**, Sammy. Maddy isn't a slouch when it comes to these robberies. In the past, she's been able to **lock down** entire museums, counter security measures without **breaking a sweat**, and leave without much trouble. For the *Girl with a Pearl Earring*, she'll **pull out all the stops**."

"Don't forget that Eric's somewhere out there."

Darla nods. "And there's also that. If Eric's been caught, then he could be a hostage. They're probably **onto us**. They know there are people here who could turn this robbery into a real mess for them. They'll be waiting."

Emily **stands up** and taps Darla on the shoulder. "I am a little familiar with how the security works with the painting," Emily says. "The museum installed something, a metal case that comes up from the floor and surrounds the frame. In addition, metal bars fall from the ceiling around the exhibit."

"Interesting. I remember reading something about that," you say. "The case seals the painting in a thick metal sleeve—actually, almost like a tight box. Even if they cut through the bars around the exhibit, it will be **next to impossible** for them to get the painting out of the case."

Darla **thinks hard** for a moment. "There is a way. If I know about it, then Maddy will know it too."

You feel hopeful. "But if she tries to cut through the metal case, she could cut through the painting. It would be worthless."

Darla waves her arms excitedly. "They won't cut through the case," she says. "Once they remove the metal bars, they'll switch from cutting tools to magnets—powerful ones—that can slide the locks on the case **out of place**."

"That means we must hurry," Emily says, panic in her eyes.

Darla looks around at your ragtag group with doubt. "We need to get help," she says. "You've been stripped of your walkie-talkies, and my phone hasn't worked ever since the alarms **went off**."

"One of us must go outside of the museum and find help while the rest of us **slows down** the thieves," suggests Emily.

Jean raises his hand. "I will volunteer."

Emily and Georges nod. "Jean knows this place better than anyone. He will find an exit and alert the local police."

"Be careful around the main entrance," you tell Jean. "The rogue security guards are **crawling all over the place**."

Jean gives you a **thumbs-up** and leaves.

"Let's go," Darla says, clapping her hands. "Let's save our girl."

Emily and Georges lead you both to a utility closet where you grab some broomsticks, rope, and metal flashlights. The four of you form a strange team as you **make your way** to the main exhibit. Unlike the rest of the museum, the gallery there is bustling with activity. The noise from the power tools **cuts through the air** and **makes a racket**.

"We have to hurry," Emily points out. "They are almost through the metal bars."

True enough, the thieves have begun to remove the bars surrounding the painting.

You watch closely, counting the number of thieves. There are about nine thieves in all moving about. Three sit near the entrance, laughing and resting, while two more carry the metal bars away from the work site. Maddy stands in the back, overseeing the whole operation. One other thief, a beefy man, accompanies her like a personal bodyguard.

When the last of the metal bars is removed, two other men carry large circular pads to the exhibit. They stand in front of the *Girl with a Pearl Earring* and attach the pads to the metal case. Then, moving in slow, circular motions, the men drag the pads over and over the metal surface.

Darla **looks on** in admiration. "I've got to **hand it to Maddy**. She came fully prepared. Her men are manually sliding the locks **out of place** now."

The metal case around the painting falls away in pieces to reveal the painted canvas. The criminals continue to drop the metal plates with the magnets until the *Girl with a Pearl Earring* is fully exposed. Maddy claps her hands in triumph and then orders the men to remove the painting from its frame.

"I cannot stand here and watch this," Emily says, **standing up**.

"No, Emily! *Attendez!*" Georges warns.

But it is too late. Emily bolts for the painting. The three rogue guards at the entrance stand as Emily races by them.

"*S'éloigner de la peinture!*" Emily shouts.

"**Heads up**, people! Looks like we have company," one of the thieves shouts to the rest of the crew.

"Who let the guards out?" another yells in surprise.

One of Maddy's men confronts Emily with a gun. "**Hold it right there!**"

Emily **stands her ground**, seemingly daring the thief to shoot. "All fake!" she screams. Before the man can react, Emily swings her stick and hits the fake weapon out of his hand.

You look over at Maddy who calmly orders the thieves at the painting to continue working. The rest of her group **set their sights on you**.

"**Watch out!**" Darla shouts, just as one thief rushes at you.

The impact sends you both sliding on the slick marble floor, but you manage to get up first. With a loud **battle cry**, you swing your weapon over your head and beat your attacker back until he **cries uncle** and surrenders.

"Sammy!" someone shouts.

You look up to see someone running into the skirmish wearing a suit of armor. The knight flips open his helmet.

"Eric! Where did you come from?"

"So glad to see you guys," he says, wielding a sword.

"Behind you!" you yell as an attacker lunges.

Eric **spins on his heels** and hits the thief **square in** the jaw with the sword's pommel. "**Taste metal!**" Eric yells.

The goon falls to the floor. Eric puts his foot on the man's chest and hoists his sword high in the air. "I am Sir Eric!" he bellows.

You **roll your eyes** and smile at your ridiculous but brave friend. In seconds, Eric flips down the visor on his helmet and **rushes off** to help Georges.

Meanwhile, you scan the room for Maddy. The *Girl with a Pearl Earring* has been removed from its frame now and is being **rolled up**. One of the criminals places it inside a leather tube and **hands it over** to Maddy. She looks at it triumphantly and slings it over her shoulder.

"Darla!" you scream.

Darla sees Maddy and runs after her, her stick raised in the air. Maddy stands there, **coolheaded** and wearing a strange smile. Just before Darla reaches her, Maddy's large bodyguard steps in front of her and absorbs the blows from Darla's weapon with his chest. Darla hits him several times with her broomstick, **raining down blow after blow**, but the giant man doesn't seem to react to her attack at all.

"That all you got?" the massive thief says, unfazed.

Darla pauses to **catch her breath**. She is nearly **doubled-over** in exhaustion. "I've got **a few more moves**," she yells back.

When she **straightens up** again, the man moves forward to grab her. Darla drops to the ground and sweeps her leg at his feet to topple him over. To her shock, the towering guard just laughs as the kick does nothing. She tries another low, sweeping kick, trying to get him off-balance, but he stays upright.

Through the commotion, you glimpse Maddy quickly gathering her things. She **looks out** at the galleries and scans for an opening. Then, with the poise of a cat, the master thief **makes a run for it**.

Darla is shouting frantically at you. "Sammy," she yells. "You'll **have the inside track** if you **head her off** before she gets to the Main Hall!"

If you decide to chase after Maddy inside the galleries and catch her *before* she reaches the Main Hall, go to **page 206**.

If you decide to skip the galleries and go to the Mall Hall directly and wait to catch Maddy there by surprise, go to **page 212**.

Maddy believes you are going to try to break something to cause a distraction. You don't wait for her to react. You **walk over** to a shelf with a set of coffee mugs on it, grab the largest one, and **throw it down** on the floor. When the mug shatters, you can't help but flinch.

Maddy raises an eyebrow. "That's something I didn't expect," she comments. "But you're kind of cute when you're angry."

Without her big black coat on, Maddy looks smaller and less intimidating. She doesn't seem to be carrying any other weapons.

*Wrong move. I should have **taken her** while I had the chance!*

You wonder if it is now too late to **make a fast break**. Maddy's associates have now arrived at the gift shop to join her. Willie grabs your arm and spins you around, pinning you against the wall. You look at Maddy for help.

Maddy seems to sense your distress. "Keep this one intact, please," she orders Willie. "We may need a hostage. Do I **make myself clear**?"

Go to **page 112**.

You decide to chase after Maddy through the maze of galleries. You reason that if you run fast enough, you can **cut her off** and reach her before she even finds a way back to the Main Hall.

*I'll **head her off** before she gets there.*

You exit the main exhibit and enter a section of interconnected galleries. Each gallery has several openings leading to other rooms, but most entrances have been **blocked off**. Only a select few galleries have entrances where the security gates haven't been **lowered down** completely. The museum is a maze of **dead-ends**.

Your ears **perk up**. Nearby, you can hear the sound of Maddy's heels echoing on the marble floor. You try to follow the patter of footsteps, but just when you think you have **picked up her trail**, you **hit a wall**. You keep finding yourself entering galleries with security gates blocking your path. After a few bad turns, you eventually reach a hallway that leads into a smaller set of galleries.

Unsure where you are now, frustration **sets in**, and you start to **kick yourself**. It would have been easier to go to the main entrance from the main exhibit, making a **beeline** through the East Wing. All galleries eventually connect to the Main Hall.

Up ahead, you hear footsteps coming your way. You **crouch down** and prepare to tackle the person. When you see who it is, you **breathe a sigh of relief**.

"Where's Maddy?" Darla shouts.

"Sorry, Darla. I **dropped the ball** on this," you say. "I thought I could **sneak up** on her from behind, but I lost her in this maze. I should have just gone to the Main Hall directly and stopped her there."

You and Darla **split up** for one last chance to find Maddy. Back in the Main Hall, something **catches your eye**. At the center of the room is a large fountain. You gasp when you come closer. In the fountain, sinking into the water, is Maddy's art tube.

Go to **page 215**.

It seems like a good idea to check the bathrooms; Darla could be **hiding out** there. As you enter the *toilettes*, you hear the sound of muffled coughing and **stop short**. You think it would be safer to **turn around** and leave, but then you hear a low groan coming from inside a stall.

Walking quietly to the door, you push it open. Inside is a terrified museum worker, bound and gagged by the toilet. His face appears ghostly white, and spit drools from the corners of his mouth.

"Are you okay?" you ask. You recognize the man from earlier. He is the attendant who scolded you while you were in line to see the *Girl with a Pearl Earring.*

He begins to breathe faster when you crouch down to help him. The tape over his mouth **comes off** easily enough, though it causes him some pain.

"*Qui êtes-vous?* Who are you?" the flustered attendant asks.

"A *tourist-i-que*. Tourist."

"*Touristique?*" The man peers at you and then suddenly recognizes your face. "You . . . you!" He looks shocked. "What you are doing? It is not safe! Not safe!" The man's face **turns red** as his whole body **tenses up** against his restraints.

"Relax. I'm here to help. Let me see."

The knots around his legs, chest, and hands **take a moment** to unravel; his captors **tied him up** tight. When he is released, the man groans in relief as he rubs his wrists chafed raw from the tape.

Then, without warning, he slams you against the wall, sticking his forearm against your throat and choking you.

"*Voleur!*" he shouts. "I should have known."

"What?" you gasp, shocked at his sudden rage.

Seething, he hisses, "You are one of the thieves!"

"I'm not a thief. **Come on**! I just let you go!"

His arm stays locked under your chin, and you gasp and choke for air. As you struggle, he **looks you directly in the eye**, grunting and breathing heavily. You meet his stare, hoping he will believe you.

"I'm not a *voleur*," you state forcefully, pointing at yourself. "I am *touristique*."

Though your body shakes with nerves, you feel a sense of pride **standing up** for yourself. With all you have been through already, and what you will likely have to go through before the day is done, you feel a surge of confidence.

The attendant releases his grip and stares at you. You can tell he is trying to **make sense** of the situation. You **lean back** against the stall wall, **meeting his glare** with one of your own. The tense standoff ends when you both hear the door to the bathrooms open. Someone steps inside. The man instinctively reaches for his nightstick that is no longer there.

Footsteps echo on the tile floor. The stall door **swings open**. Standing in front of you is someone holding a vase by its neck, ready to swing it like a baseball bat. As it hurtles through the air, the attendant catches the vase with both hands, stopping it before it smashes into his face. He **pulls away** the pottery and **pushes off** the attacker.

The person is down on the floor, and you **get a better look**. "Darla?" you gasp.

You grab the attendant and pull him back before he can attack your friend. Surprised, he clutches at your chest and then pushes you back against the stall wall. Eyes wide, he begins to shout at you in French and shoves you against the tile wall several more times, **knocking the wind out of you**.

All the while, Darla pleads for him to let you go. "Calm down!" she cries, pulling at the man's arm. She tries again in French.

The next few seconds are tense as all three of you **shout over** each other. Suddenly, the attendant bellows something and lets you go. You all collapse on the floor in a tired heap.

"It's you, Sammy! I can't believe it," Darla says, putting her arms around you.

"Are you okay?" you ask, holding her for a few seconds.

The attendant **clears his throat**.

Darla reaches inside her shirt and **pulls out** something strapped to her waist. She **takes out** a badge and **holds it up** to the man's face. "I'm with Interpol," she tells him. "And he's **with me**."

You and the attendant stare in shock at the identification card.

Darla shrugs and sighs. "I guess it's time to **spill the beans**. The truth is I'm not really a tourist. I'm an agent hunting a thief who went into hiding years ago. We **got word** she was active again, so I've been traveling across Europe looking for **leads**."

You search for the words. "What—why? How? This whole time?" you mumble, clearly confused. "Why didn't you just tell us?"

"For all I knew, you and Eric might have been working with her, so I had to **stay undercover**. Madeleine de Castellano has a network of thieves who bring in other criminals into her various teams. That's how she recruits. She's also known for bribing museum staff and getting the workers to help her."

"Madeleine?" you say.

The attendant interrupts, **pushing you aside**. "*Vous êtes avec* Interpol?"

"*Oui*," Darla responds. "*Et vous?*"

"My name is Jean," the man says. You all shake hands.

"Now that we're all acquainted, it's time we get you to safety," she says, looking at you. "Jean and I will work together to secure the painting."

"I'm not going anywhere," you tell Darla. "I want to help."

"No, Sammy," Darla says sternly. "I've been dedicated to this case, and I can't have you **ruining my chances** of catching de Castellano."

Looks can be deceiving. You see another side of Darla that you have never seen before—a **far cry** from the sweet and outgoing artist who has been traveling with you.

"I can help, you know," you say, a little hurt.

"Actually, what are you still doing here? And where's Eric? Please don't tell me you're both **playing heroes** trying to **save the day**."

"It's a bit more, uh, complicated than that," you tell her. "Do we even have time for me to explain?" You smile sheepishly and scratch your head.

"Idiots," Darla says, chuckling. "My sweet, brave idiots. Well, do you have any information that can help us?"

You start at the beginning, explaining how you lost the tour group and met a woman named Maddy while in line for the *Girl with a Pearl Earring*. You notice that Jean snorts at this, probably remembering how you **held up** the line.

"Describe her for me."

You give Darla a description of Maddy.

"A thin woman wearing a heavy black coat? Sounds like her," Darla says, clearly impressed. "Congratulations, Sammy. You met Madeleine de Castellano and **lived to tell the tale**."

You wonder whether you should gloat or **count your blessings**.

"Do you know how many are working with her?" Darla asks.

"Security guards, henchmen, random crew members. I don't have an exact number, but there's more of them than you'd think."

Darla nods knowingly. "One of Maddy's goons and I played a little **game of cat and mouse** for a while before I gave him a really bad headache. I had to **split his head open** with a vase in one of the galleries." Darla looks apologetically at the attendant. "Sorry. I hope it wasn't worth too much."

Jean just shrugs.

"And what's your story, *monsieur*?" Darla asks the man. You listen to Jean as he tells his story.

"I did not know about today's robbery until things started **going downhill**. I was not even scheduled to work today, but I made a mistake and came anyway."

Darla scratches her forehead, trying to **make sense of it all**. "This operation is quite complex, and it must have taken months to prepare. Her crew must have **wormed their way** into the museum."

Jean nods. "There were **new faces** today."

"New hires," Darla guesses. "Maddy and her crew must have **fixed the schedule** in their favor and bribed a few of the older employees to **turn on** the rest during the heist."

"I was **tied up** by a coworker who said Maddy promised him a lot of money. His wife just had a baby, and he needed the cash."

Darla sighs. "That's how Maddy gets them. She uses their vulnerabilities, their **soft spots**, and she promises a **big payday**."

"Are there any other people still **tied up**?" you ask Jean.

"Not many, I think," Jean replies. "Like I said, I did not recognize most of the other attendants and guards on the floor today."

"They could all be Maddy's people," Darla warns. "If we do find any other loyal museum employees, it would only be a **handful**."

"We should check then," you suggest. "There's the women's bathroom next to this one and plenty of other places they could have hidden people."

The three of you go to the other bathroom where, fortunately enough, you find a museum guard, bound and gagged like Jean was. As Jean unties the guard, Darla questions him and translates.

"He heard us talking in the other bathroom, but he was too afraid to make any noise. His name is Georges."

"Well, he's safe with us now," you say. You and Georges shake hands.

"There's **power in numbers**," Darla says, agreeing. "We should go find more of the guards."

Go to **page 199**.

You leave the room and go directly to the Main Hall. Darla is right. It is probably best to forego the maze of galleries altogether and **cut her off** directly at the Main Hall where she will eventually have to pass through. Depending on how well Maddy navigates the galleries and how many turns she makes along the way, you calculate you can beat her to the Main Hall and **head her off** there.

Just as you anticipated, Maddy comes out of a gallery and enters the Main Hall. She jogs into the open, the tube container that holds the painting bouncing on her shoulder. You notice that she is wearing her oversized black coat again, and keeps fumbling with it as she runs. You **race toward her**, but Maddy hears you coming and speeds away.

"Maddy! You're not leaving with that painting!" you shout.

Maddy moves through the open area, cornering around large sculptures and pulling down the rows of busts onto the floor. You nimbly jump over the debris and obstacles like mini-hurdles, until you reach her at the room's centerpiece: a small fountain with a miniature pond.

"**Hand it over**," you demand, breathing hard. "You're **done**, Maddy."

Maddy sticks her hand in the fountain and splashes water on her face to cool off. She then delicately pulls the tube from around her shoulders and **pops off** the top.

"Sammy, you're going to have to let me go," she says.

To your shock, she casually **holds out** the tube over the water. Then, to emphasize her threat, she drops it.

"Don't!" you yell.

The tube makes a hollow sound when it **lands**, and it begins to roll dangerously toward the edge of the pond. Maddy swiftly moves forward and stops the tube with the **ball of her foot** and holds it in place with her heel.

You let out a big sigh of relief. Maddy can't seriously be considering destroying the painting, can she?

"Don't do it," you say. "You'll regret it."

Maddy laughs. "Oh, really? I will?"

"Why would you ruin it?" you exclaim. "After everything you've done today? Why would you even consider—?"

"I am the famous Madeleine de Castellano," she says, bowing dramatically. "I can do as I please."

"Except take that painting," you point out. "And you know it."

Maddy sneers and **eyes you** coldly. She **steps on** the tube and puts more weight on the painting.

"The deal is, you get the painting **safe and sound**, and I go free. Just take a few steps back," Maddy says.

"Fine," you tell her, moving back.

"Don't make any quick moves. We have a deal here. And tell your friend I'm not joking," Maddy says.

You **turn around** to see Darla holding out her Interpol badge. You can tell by her bloodied shirt and noticeable limp that she is badly injured.

"I mean it," Maddy threatens. She **makes a show** of rolling the tube back and forth on the ground with her foot.

"Madeleine de Castellano," Darla declares, her voice low and steady. "You're **under arrest**." Darla hobbles to your side.

"Stay back!" Maddy hisses at Darla. "I'd hate to see you lose the thing most precious to you."

From here, you can see water splashing all over the tube.

"**Look at yourself**, Madeleine," Darla says quietly. "Look at what you've become. You wouldn't dare ruin that painting. You'd lose all the respect you've gained."

Maddy chuckles to herself. "I can **start over** with a new name if it **comes to that**. Let me go, and you get the painting. It's simple. Then we can go back to playing our game of international **hide and seek**."

"Sorry, but I'm not **buying it**," Darla says.

"You have no imagination. You're too stupid to see that I **hold**

all the cards," Maddy scoffs. "I'm a genius. A genius! I'm always going to be **two steps ahead**."

"You're a **clever bird**, I'll admit that," Darla says. "But don't **overshoot the mark** on this."

Maddy smiles and narrows her eyes. "It's not that simple, you know. You think I'm overshooting, but I'm just aiming for another target."

With a swift kick from her pointed boot, the tube with the painting inside jumps the lip of the pond and falls into the water. Maddy gleefully **bolts away** as you stare in shock at the ruined painting.

Darla moves to chase after her, but her injured leg **gives out**. "The painting!" she cries out. "Maddy!"

If you decide to go to the fountain and save the painting, go to **page 215**.

If you decide to run after Maddy and stop her from getting away, go to **page 218**.

You stoop down to **pick up** the tube from the water. Smooth and light, the leather case is all that is left of Maddy, and you expect the worst as you look inside.

"Oh, no. Is it . . . ?" Darla asks, her voice **trailing off**. "Please tell me the painting is alright, Sammy."

You are **struck dumb** as you stare inside the container. "**Good news and bad news**," you say. "The good news is that the painting isn't damaged."

"The bad news?"

"The bad news is that the painting isn't damaged because it's not in here."

"What?"

You shake the container. "There was nothing inside."

Darla starts to run toward the galleries, but you **pull her back**. "Maddy's gone," you say. "And the painting too. She must have taken it with her. I'm so sorry."

Angry tears fill Darla's eyes, and you try to comfort her. Together, you trudge back to the main exhibit where you find the rest of your allies. Their eyes brighten at the sight of the leather casing, but you shake your head and explain that the painting is gone.

"Are you sure?" Eric asks, confused.

You hand the empty tube over to Emily who takes it with both hands. "Oh, no," Emily says, after looking at the case.

"We tried," Darla says. "We got close. Unfortunately, Maddy **got the better of us**."

Eric scowls and looks down at the floor. Darla pulls herself away and shows him her badge.

"Interpol?" he exclaims. "I thought you were . . . Wait—does that mean you won't **go out with me** then?"

Darla smiles sweetly. "You're a nice guy, Eric, but **not really my type**. Sorry."

"Wow," Eric says. Then his face brightens. "An Interpol agent just **brushed me off**. How cool is that!"

"I should have told you and Sammy sooner. It might have helped. I came to Lyon to **track down** these art thieves."

Darla looks at the group of captured thieves.

"This doesn't look like all of them," you observe.

"Some have escaped," Georges says grimly.

Darla kneels in front of one of the thieves. "Where will Maddy go with the painting?"

He laughs in her face. "Who knows? The Bahamas. The Caymans. Singapore. Malta. **Your guess is as good as mine.**"

Darla grabs the man by the hair and yanks, pulling his face closer to hers, but the thief continues to laugh.

"What do we do now?" you ask.

"There's nothing we can do," she says angrily. "All we can do is wait for the local authorities to arrive. As for Maddy, we try to remain patient and **bide our time**. She'll try to sell the painting in the near-future. She'll likely **make a killing** on the black market. We'll have our agents check every auction house, **underground** or **legit**, though it will be like **searching for a needle in a haystack**."

Georges looks at Emily and speaks. "We still have our jobs as guards. We will walk through the museum and see what else has been taken or damaged."

"Oh, yeah, about that . . ." you say, remembering all the items you damaged or destroyed along the way.

You want to apologize, but Georges and Emily look at you blankly. They wait for Darla to respond, but she remains silent, **lost in thought**. They wave at you and leave just as quietly.

Eric walks over and puts his arm around your shoulders. "**Look on the bright side**," he says. "We're alive at least. And the museum will survive. Insurance will **take care** of the damages."

You nod halfheartedly. "I guess you're right, but she's out there somewhere with that priceless painting."

Darla puts her hands on your shoulders. "You did more than anyone could ask of you," she says. "Not bad for a couple of kids fresh out of college. And I'm now closer to finding Maddy than I've ever been. All because of you."

"Thanks," you respond shyly. You still feel uneasy about the loss of the painting and all of the other artifacts. "I guess there's a **silver lining** to all this."

"You have to admire Maddy's plan though," Eric says. "Even I couldn't have **come up** with a scheme that ingenious."

"Oh, please, Eric," Darla says, chuckling. "It's obvious you **don't have the brains** for something this complicated. Sometimes I think we're **no match** for the infamous Madeleine de Castellano."

"Well, that's why we have Sammy here," Eric tells her. "He's our secret weapon. He could have **come up** with something equally brilliant."

You shrug sheepishly.

"An art student turned art thief," Darla says, considering the idea. "Now that would be an impressive **turn of events**, almost as impressive as this **artful heist**."

THE END

You decide to run after Maddy and stop her from getting away. Everything moves in slow motion as your body **springs into action**. You can see the tube floating on the surface of the pond, **filling up** with water through its open side. The painting is likely ruined already. Soon, it will sink, and the painting will be submerged. You fight the urge to stop and scoop it out. Your focus returns to catching the woman who did this.

Maddy can't get away with this. I won't let her.

Your muscles are **telling you** to run. You **race around** the fountain and try to **cut off** Maddy's escape.

When she sees you, Maddy **turns on her heels** and **loses her footing**. She tries to **get up** to run, but you pounce on her before she has a chance. She spins as you grab her shoulder and hits you in the chest. You fall and bring Maddy down with you. On the floor, she claws at you, but you grab her wrists and pin them behind her back. Darla rushes to your side and helps you restrain her.

"No!" the thief screams. "How stupid can you be? You let the *Girl with a Pearl Earring* drown in a pond?"

To your confusion, she starts to laugh. Has Maddy **gone mad**? Her hysterics echo through the museum.

Darla reaches into the pond and **holds up** the drenched tube. She shakes it, and water pours out of it—but nothing else.

"What?" you gasp.

Darla grimaces. "There's nothing else inside."

Maddy continues to laugh.

"Where is it?" you demand.

Maddy tightens her mouth and shrugs. "**Beats me.**" But then you notice her eyes. She is looking down nervously at the buttons of her coat . . . her huge black coat.

"The coat!" you cry.

You hold Maddy down as Darla unzips her black coat and removes it. She **holds it up** and shakes it. "There's nothing here, Sammy," Darla says, disappointed.

"What?" you say. "No. It can't be. I don't understand." Suddenly, you remember something. "Wait. Check the lining!" you tell her. "There should be a tear somewhere."

Maddy stops smiling. Panic spreads across her face. Her green eyes are stricken with fear.

Darla rips apart the coat's inner lining. Sure enough, hidden inside the lining in the sleeve is the *Girl with a Pearl Earring*.

"You literally had it **hidden up your sleeve**," you say, **under your breath**.

"Hmph," Maddy grunts back. "**Whistle-blower**."

As you bring Maddy back to the main exhibit, Eric and the other guards **on your side** greet you with smiles and cheers. The **reign** of Madeleine de Castellano has finally **come to an end**. She looks defeated; an angry scowl is etched across her face. The thieves and some of the corrupt security guards have been **tied up**. Your allies look a little **beat up**, but it is okay. **Nothing beats** saving the painting and catching a fugitive art thief; it is worth the bumps and bruises.

"Hopefully, she'll help us **track down** the other paintings she has stolen over the years," Darla says.

"How did you know?" Eric asks after you tell him the story.

"I **had a hunch**," you respond. "When I first met Maddy, one of the things I noticed about her was her big black coat. Why should such a tiny woman need such a big coat? She wasn't wearing it when we started the fight with her crew earlier, but when she was **making her escape**, I noticed she had **put it on** again."

"Clever," Darla comments.

"But not clever enough for my buddy—the world's greatest detective!" Eric declares, slapping you on the back.

Darla gives him a **dry look**, and Eric laughs. "And the world's greatest Interpol agent!" he adds, squeezing Darla's arm.

"You did it, Sammy," Darla says.

"*We* did it," you tell her.

"We're heroes!" Eric shouts out loud, and everyone laughs.

You turn to **take a look** at the painting, which Emily has unrolled and placed over Maddy's black coat.

"What do you think she was thinking when Vermeer was painting her?" Emily asks.

The question **hangs in the air**, and you all stare at the portrait with wordless wonder.

While the security guards go off into the museum to survey the damage, you wait with Darla for the local police to **show up**. News crews soon descend upon the museum, and they surround you as the police escort you out. One of the reporters gets Darla in front of a camera. You notice how poised she looks **under the lights**.

Frankie, Barrett, and Willie come out one by one, escorted by several police officers. Willie **screams at the top of his lungs** when he sees Darla. "I knew it! I knew she was Interpol! I knew it!"

You smile when the thieves are packed away in the police vans.

Jean, Georges, and Emily are also **taken away** for questioning, but Darla tells you, "I'll **take care of them**. They helped us so much. They should get medals."

Eventually, the police **bring out** Maddy. You almost pity her. The mastermind looks frazzled and **keeps her head down**. Her normally sleek head of hair is **all over the place**. When a reporter asks to see her face, Maddy tosses her head back, revealing a look of defeat. Her once pristine mascara and red lipstick are now smeared.

"*Raton laveur!*" some children chant as they point at her.

"What does that mean?"

"Raccoon," Darla translates.

You chuckle, and Maddy's eyes **hone in** on you like lasers. You freeze as she looks at you with a strange stare. Something is very, very wrong.

"No," you say. "Stop!"

You run to the woman. You stare intently at the woman's eyes. Now, you know **for sure**.

"What's wrong, Sammy?"

"This isn't Maddy."

"What? Of course it is," she replies. "We **tied her up** together. The police have her in custody."

"No, look again."

Darla **walks up** to the thief and **pulls away** her hair. Darla begins to shout in French and questions the police escorts. She is still arguing with them when a flood of reporters comes your way.

The cameras **turn their attention** to you, and the reporters shove their microphones in your face. You stutter, trying to answer their questions. Awkwardly, you tell them, "I don't speak French." Everyone around you laughs. One reporter introduces himself and asks you in English, "What is your name?"

Before you can say anything, Eric pushes his way between you and the microphone, and you step back as Eric **takes the spotlight**. "This, folks, is my man, Sammy. He's the one who saved the *Girl with a Pearl Earring*!" Eric shouts.

Camera flashes blind you, and the people **burst into applause**. Several Interpol agents **carry out** the painting and **hold it up** next to you for the cameras. It has been returned to its frame and looks as stunning as ever. You smile awkwardly as the photographers **take their snapshots**.

Darla comes to your side and whispers in your ear. "It's not her."

You wince. "How did she **slip from our grasp**?"

"Someone posing as an Interpol agent probably got the police to **hand her over**. She used a **double**. Her **fall guy**—er, woman."

"Classic move. What do we do now?"

"Nothing," Darla says. "**Enjoy the spotlight**. The police will **take you in** for questioning, but I'll vouch for you. For now, celebrate the fact that we didn't lose the painting."

"And what will you do?"

Darla sighs bitterly. "Keep looking for her. She's out there somewhere, planning another heist, **keeping one step ahead of us**."

Darla embraces you in a long hug and then leaves. She enters a car, waves at you and Eric, and drives away.

The reporters have begun to ask you more questions, and you turn to look at the painting again. Earlier today, hordes of people wanted their chance to **get up close and personal** to the painting. You stare deeply into the girl's eyes and begin to wonder what the young Dutch girl really must have been thinking all those years ago as she sat to be painted by Johannes Vermeer.

"You will return home with extraordinary memories," a reporter observes. "What will the painting remind you of?"

"Where do I begin?" you stammer.

Eric laughs. "Well, as they say, **a picture is worth a thousand words.**"

You look at one of the video cameras. The **whole world is watching**.

"It's a long story. Let me start at the beginning," you say. You **pick your words** carefully as you tell them the story of your **close call** with the infamous Madeleine de Castellano.

THE END

[GLOSSARY]

THE GLOSSARY DEFINES the phrases and expressions that are tested in the decision points throughout the book.

a few cards short of a full deck: an expression used to indicate that a person is not very smart or bright

back to square one: an expression that indicates one must start over again because something isn't working well or needs to be changed or tweaked

ball's in your court: to give someone the power to make a decision or to ask someone to make a choice

better the devil you know than the devil you don't know: an expression used to imply that between two bad choices, it is better to choose the option that you are more familiar with

biting off more than you can chew: to take on a burden or responsibility that may be overwhelming

come to grips: to deal with a problem or situation proactively; to have a realization about some circumstance

cut her off: to stop someone from doing something or reaching a destination, usually in a pursuit (see also: **head her off**)

cut out for this: to have the stamina or willpower to handle a situation

cut to the chase: to take the direct route; to get to the main point, argument, or purpose

deliver the goods: to achieve an intended goal or target; to complete a task or activity

don't hold your breath: an expression used to indicate that you mustn't keep waiting for an event to happen (implying that the event is unlikely to occur)

drop it: to stop a course of action or to cease doing a task

even out the odds: to make things more fair and equitable; to make things less risky and dangerous

faced with: to be confronted by something or someone

get it down to a fine art: to perfect something with planning or practice

get my hands dirty: to participate in something directly

give an arm and a leg: an expression used to indicate that one would pay a lot of money for something

go off the deep end: an expression used to describe that a situation is getting serious or dire

Glossary

go off the rails: to act impulsively

go-getter: a person who is self-motivated and bold

goes dead: to run out of a power source or energy; to be broken or not working

going for broke: to exert the maximum effort to achieve a goal or task; to give it your best effort

got a few tricks up my sleeve: an expression used to indicate that one has a solution or has come up with an idea

got a handle on it: to have control over something

got real: an expression used to show that a situation is getting serious or deserves special attention

hand it over: to relinquish something to someone

have it your way: an expression used to tell someone they can do whatever they want to do

head her off: to stop someone from doing something or reaching a destination, usually in a pursuit (see also: **cut her off**)

in the same boat: to be in the same situation or similar circumstances as someone else

make a fast break: to escape

pick up your feet: to quicken one's pace or to hurry

put one over on me: to be tricked or fooled by someone

show you who's boss: an expression used when one wants to assert authority or dominance, usually in situations of retaliation

take care of it: to manage something; to kill off something and get rid of it; alternatively, to protect and care for something

take matters into our own hands: to be assertive; to take a course of action directly

taken for a ride: to be fooled or deceived; to be taken advantage of

window of opportunity: a rare or special opportunity

[ACKNOWLEDGMENTS]

I want to thank, with resounding appreciation, my editor Adam Collins. I also want to thank Genevieve DeGuzman at Night Owls Press, and Karen Hannah, O Captain, my Captain.

To the teachers who kept pushing me to continue writing, you gave me a voice. Thank you Ms. Babczak (Salinas High), Professor Kevin Clark (Cal Poly SLO), Professor Maria Teutsch (Hartnell), and George Ramos (Cal Poly SLO).

[ABOUT THE AUTHOR]

JACOB JUN was born in Pusan, South Korea and has called California his home since his family emigrated there in the early 1980s. Growing up with video games, grunge music, and comic books, Jacob became an avid reader and geek, and those passions have followed him all over the world as he took up jobs as a teacher, writer, and editor. He now works as a photographer and writer based out of Salinas, and his experiences have helped him see the world as an artful place. .

[ABOUT THE PUBLISHER]

NIGHT OWLS PRESS (nightowlspress.com) is a small, independent press that publishes nonfiction books that challenge and re-imagine prevailing conventions about business, work, and life. Covering topics on entrepreneurship, education, innovation, and social responsibility, its focus is to turn big ideas into great books that inform and inspire.

Find out more about Night Owls Press books at www.nightowlspress.com/e-book-store/. For special orders and bulk purchases, contact admin@nightowlspress.com.

[ABOUT THE SERIES]

TURN OF PHRASE ESL (TOP ESL) is the first-ever educational series that introduces English language learners to idioms, phrasal verbs, and collocations in the form of chooseable path novels. TOP ESL is designed for intermediate to advanced level young adult and adult learners.

Find out more about the series at www.nightowlspress.com/turn-of-phrase-esl/ or visit www.nightowlspress.com/e-book-store/ and search for TOP ESL titles. For orders or to request a series catalog, contact admin@nightowlspress.com.

Available titles:

An Artful Heist by Jacob Jun
Blackout by G.K. Gilbert
Cleaning House by Rebecca M. Karli
The Spoonmaker's Diamond by Mary M. Slechta

CPSIA information can be obtained at www.ICGtesting.com
Printed in the USA
LVOW08s0031140716

496107LV00002B/33/P